Supporting Young Children Through Change and Everyday Transitions

Practical Strategies for Practitioners and Parents

Sonia Mainstone-Cotton

Jessica Kingsley Publishers
London and Philadelphia

First published in 2020
by Jessica Kingsley Publishers
73 Collier Street
London N1 9BE, UK
and
400 Market Street, Suite 400
Philadelphia, PA 19106, USA

www.jkp.com

Library of Congress Cataloging in Publication Data
A CIP catalog record for this book is available from the Library of Congress

British Library Cataloguing in Publication Data
A CIP catalogue record for this book is available from the British Library

ISBN 978 1 78775 158 3
eISBN 978 1 78775 159 0

Printed and bound in Great Britain

Supporting Young Children Through Change and Everyday Transitions

by the same author

Listening to Young Children in Early Years Settings
A Practical Guide
Sonia Mainstone-Cotton
ISBN 978 1 78592 469 9
eISBN 978 1 78450 855 5

Promoting Emotional Wellbeing in Early Years Staff
A Practical Guide for Looking after Yourself and Your Colleagues
Sonia Mainstone-Cotton
ISBN 978 1 78592 335 7
eISBN 978 1 78450 656 8

Promoting Young Children's Emotional Health and Wellbeing
A Practical Guide for Professionals and Parents
Sonia Mainstone-Cotton
ISBN 978 1 78592 054 7
eISBN 978 1 78450 311 6

Can I tell you about Bipolar Disorder?
A Guide for Friends, Family and Professionals
Sonia Mainstone-Cotton
Illustrated by Jon Birch
ISBN 978 1 78592 470 5
eISBN 978 1 78450 854 8
Can I tell you about...? series

of related interest

Supporting Vulnerable Children in the Early Years
Practical Guidance and Strategies for Working with Children at Risk
Edited by Pat Beckley
Foreword by Professor Chris Atkin
ISBN 978 1 78592 237 4
eISBN 978 1 78450 515 8

*Thank you to Ruth, Fred, Andy, Sharon and Kieran,
working and learning with you all in the Nurture Outreach
team has taught me so much. For the four years I have
supported teachers and TAs, it has been a privilege to
journey with you through your school transitions.*

*Thank you to Donna Gaywood and Debbie Harvey
for their contributions to Chapter 6, and to Louisa
Tickner for her contribution to Chapter 7.*

*Thanks to Will, Fred and Louie for reading,
advising and offering thoughts.*

Contents

Introduction

Change is part of everyone's life, and some of us manage change better than others. Some people thrive on change, they love the variety and become very bored when things stay the same; others love similarity, they are at their happiest when there is routine, familiarity, sameness. This book is about helping children manage and cope with changes and transitions. Children experience numerous changes throughout the day and in their young lives. Some children, like adults, are relaxed and at ease with change; others can find change very distressing. This book will look at some simple but effective ways in which we can support children through changes.

Before we continue, I want you to make a moment and think about how you manage change. I think it is helpful to be reflective about how we feel about change. Below are a few questions to help you think about this.

Questions for practice

Do you have a routine in your day that you like to stick to? If this changes unexpectedly, how do you feel?

Are you someone who likes to live in the same house/do the same job for a number of years, or are you someone who prefers to move jobs/houses regularly?

Are you someone who gets bored easily and likes to try new things regularly, or are you someone who, once you have found something you like, sticks with it?

What helps you deal with change? Being prepared and thinking through what might happen? Or are you someone who is happy to try, experience and be in the moment with change?

These are some very simple questions, but I hope they will give you some thoughts about how you feel about change, and how you approach change. Being aware of how we feel about and deal with change in ourselves can help us to understand and reflect on how children manage change. As adults, we can often have a large amount of control over the change we experience; not always, of course, but we can usually choose the work we do, the house we live in, the food we eat, if and where we go on holiday, the friends we have, where and how we play and rest. As adults, we usually make these decisions for young children and we don't always prepare them for the changes they encounter. Some children can find this overwhelming and very scary, and then they communicate this to us through behaviours that we often describe as challenging. But if they are scared and frightened and confused, they are telling us in the only way they know how. When we stop and reflect, it is not really surprising that children can be overwhelmed by changes if they don't know what to expect or what is happening.

Helping children manage and cope with change has become a key part of my work life. I work part-time as a nurture consultant for a team in Bath called Threeways Brighter Futures. I am part of their Nurture Outreach Service, which is a service that supports Reception-aged children in their transition from pre-school to school, throughout their Reception year and across the transition into Year 1. These children find changes and transitions very challenging and they can easily become overwhelmed. A key part of my job is supporting staff in thinking about all the changes that are happening and how we can support these. This is always about clear communication to the child; it is about thinking ahead and anticipating, where possible, what might be a stressor for the child.

In previous books, I have written about children's wellbeing (Mainstone-Cotton 2017) and listening to children (Mainstone-Cotton 2019). This book is taking these ideas a step further. As I mentioned earlier, the main part of my role as a nurture consultant is to prepare children for transitions, for change, both big and small. I have learnt that if we take time to think through, prepare children, pre-warn them of changes, then we are making life a little easier for them and us, ultimately helping the children's and our wellbeing.

The two chapters in the first section of this book look at children's social and emotional development and how we need to support children's wellbeing. Each chapter in the second section then explores a different theme and the changes that a child may encounter; some of these may appear small, others are bigger issues. I hope this is a book that you can read through but also go back to and dip in and out of when a particular difficulty is arising. The themes covered are:

- new siblings

- new pets

- going on holiday

- moving home

- starting school or nursery

- family changes and separation

- illness and hospital stays

- death and bereavement.

References

Mainstone-Cotton, S. (2017) *Promoting Young Children's Emotional Health and Wellbeing: A Practical Guide for Professionals and Parents.* London: Jessica Kingsley Publishers.

Mainstone-Cotton, S. (2019) *Listening to Young Children in Early Years Settings: A Practical Guide.* London: Jessica Kingsley Publishers.

The Impact of Change on Development and Wellbeing

Chapter 1

Children's Social and Emotional Development

This chapter is going to explore how changes and transitions can have an impact on children's social and emotional development and their mental health. Most of my work life focuses on how I can help young children to have a good wellbeing, and my first book gave practical guidance on this (Mainstone-Cotton 2017). A good wellbeing is intrinsically linked to a child's social and emotional development. The more I work in this area, the more I realize that if we can equip children in their early years to be resilient, have a good wellbeing, feel safe and feel listened to, we are giving them the best start in life. Assisting children through the many changes they will encounter, and helping them to feel safe and secure though these, is a key part of supporting a child's emotional development.

Assisting children with changes and transitions is an essential part of how we support their personal, social and emotional development (PSED). We know that PSED is recognized as a crucial part of child development, which is why it is one of the three prime areas of the Early Years Foundation Stage (EYFS). There is a growing recognition of how we need to understand and attend to a child's social and emotional development. Several years ago, I went on a study trip to Sweden to see early years practice. One of the educators told us that the main focus of the work of early years practitioners in Sweden is to build and strengthen a child's PSED for the first six years of their life. Then they are ready to start building from this and begin learning other things. This approach is similar in Denmark and other Scandinavian countries. I love this approach, and it distresses me to see the focus our current government in the UK has on teaching early years reading and writing and maths over PSED.

Brain development

I firmly believe that if we can get it right with early years children we are setting them up with the best start. If we can help young children to be able to cope with change and know what it feels like to be supported through change, then this gives them a firm foundation for them to grow from and will help them to cope with later changes in their lives. To be able to do this we need to understand what is happening in a child's brain. We now understand how the brain develops; for example, the higher rational (thinking) part of the brain develops later than other parts of the brain. The reptilian (instinctive – breathing, temperature regulation, hunger, movement) and mammalian (emotional – fear, rage, but also playful and social) parts develop before the higher, rational part of the brain.

In the first few years of a child's life, the lower part of the brain dominates, such that the child can quickly come to feel overwhelmed and threatened; the higher part of the brain is not yet sufficiently developed to offer reason or to self-soothe. This is where adults need to offer soothing, comforting support to children to help them know they are safe and secure. Because of the strong and early alarm systems in a young child's brain, young children can see change and separation as a major threat. Margot Sunderland (2016) describes how the same parts of the brain are activated both when a child is distressed because of the absence of a parent and when we feel physical pain. This separation pain and separation anxiety can continue in children aged five or sometimes older (particularly older where there are attachment difficulties). It is so important that we understand this and for it to inform our practice and knowledge around supporting children with transitions. We are expecting children to make big transitions from home to nursery or childminder and then to school at a time when they are still experiencing separation as a threat and a painful experience (O'Connor 2018).

Most of my current work is in schools with children transitioning into Reception. Every year, I observe four-year-olds who are distressed at being left. Sometimes I hear staff after a few days saying words such as *'No more crying now', 'There is no need to cry'* or *'You are a big girl now, you don't need to cry.'* These are unhelpful comments; a child needs to know that their feelings have been recognized and validated, they do not need to be told to get over it. The information about how the brain perceives separation is important for teachers, teaching assistants and head teachers to hear. I think if more school staff understood this, it might alter some of the practice we have in schools and hopefully put an end to such comments.

Two schools I currently work in have newly qualified teachers in their Reception class. Both teachers said at the start of term that everyone in the class could bring in a soft, comforting toy as a transitional object. In the first weeks, the children were able to have this toy whenever they needed it. This was such a simple but powerful transitioning support for the children. We know from Winnicott's work back in 1953 that transitional objects are a tool to help children cope with separation,[1] I was really encouraged to see this long-recognized early years good practice being used by newly qualified teachers.

There is a growing recognition of the vital importance of early years practitioners having a solid understanding of brain development and neuroscience. The growth of research in these areas has enhanced our understanding in the last few years. I am not

1　www.changingminds.org/disciplines/psychoanalysis/concepts/transition_object.htm

intending to unpick or explain the subject in this book, as there are many other excellent writers who have covered it all very well. But I would recommend you take a look at this area if it is new to you:

- Anne O'Connor (2018) has an opening chapter on brain development and the impact of transitions in her book on transitions in the early years.

- Debbie Garvey (2018) has an excellent chapter looking at brain development, neuroscience and PSED; she gives a really useful introduction to the subject.

- Mine Conkbayir (2017) has a very thorough book on the subject of early childhood and neuroscience.

- Suzanne Zeedyk's website has some excellent short videos looking at brain development and how much a baby's brain develops in the first three years.[2]

Our understanding of a young child's brain development and the impact adults have on this are vital in enabling us to be aware of what we do, why we do it and how this affects a child. By having a greater understanding about this area, we are able to reflect on our practice and our decisions and have a greater awareness of how they are making a difference in children's lives. For me, having a greater understanding of neuroscience and the changes that occur in a child's brain has hugely developed my thinking and awareness in why this links with supporting children though change. PSED is such an important area for us to fully understand; if this is an area where you feel you would like to enhance your knowledge, I would recommend Kathie Brodie's latest book (2018) which has an excellent chapter focusing on PSED, exploring in detail how a child typically progresses and how, as adults, we can support this.

---

2   www.suzannezeedyk.com/videos-suzanne-zeedyk

Never too young to support a child with changes

During the almost 30 years that I have been working with children, and through being a parent, I have observed the difference it can make when a child is fully supported and appropriately informed about change. When I first started out in my career, one of my early jobs was helping children with non-organic failure to thrive (when a child is not gaining weight, unrelated to medical reasons); we supported children under the age of three (and their parents) in encouraging them to eat. We used to make video observations at the start of each piece of work, videoing mealtimes and the moments before mealtimes. Time and again, we saw children being picked up and taken to the table/high chair without any warning. Time and again the child would become very distressed and then often refuse to eat. Once we got parents to make the small change of pre-warning the child about the transition and explaining what was about to happen, the child would often be less anxious and happier during mealtime.

Right from early on in a child's life we can encourage parents to talk through changes and what is happening, from picking up a crying newborn and telling them *'I think you're hungry, let's give you some food'* or going to change a nappy, again commenting *'It's time to change your nappy.'* Starting this from birth is such an important part of preparing and helping children cope with changes. If we start out with this clear communication and support for a child, recognizing how scary something can be when change suddenly happens, by putting ourselves into our children's shoes we can begin to understand why we need to prepare them for changes right at the start of their lives.

Questions for practice

Take a moment to think about how you would feel if you were suddenly bundled into a coat, out of the house and into a car, without being told where you were going or what was happening. What feelings might that bring up in you?

Take a moment to think about all the small transitions that happen in a day with your children. How often do you tell them what is about to happen (e.g. going outside, changing activity, mealtimes, going in the car, bath time). Have you noticed a difference when you have prepared them/told them?

Adverse childhood experiences

I am sure that, for all of us, there have been key moments in our careers and learning where there have been lightbulb moments. For me, one of these key moments was watching a TED Talk by Dr Nadine Burke Harris on the subject of how childhood trauma affects health across a lifetime.[3] Her work has been dedicated to recognizing the long-term effects of childhood adversity. The children that she talks about are similar to many of the children that I and my current team have worked with, children who have experienced stresses and adversity in their early childhood. These are children who may have experienced parent mental illness, substance misuse, neglect, abuse. She talks about the vital importance of recognizing and understanding what the children have experienced and the impact this has on their lives. Nadine has recently written a book on this subject called *The Deepest Well* (Burke Harris 2018), and one of the areas she explores is the impact stress has on the brain. One aspect that I found particularly useful to understand is that if we have repeatedly experienced stressors, the amygdala (the brain's fear centre) becomes overactive, which can cause an exaggerated response to situations; it can also send out false alarms about what is scary. We might see this in a child who is becoming overwhelmed and distressed at having to move from one activity to another, or in a child who is becoming overly scared when they are visiting a doctor.

3   www.youtube.com/watch?v=95ovIJ3dsNk

Most of you reading this book will not be working with a huge number of children who have regularly experienced trauma, but you will all be working with some children who have experienced this. It is so vital for us to be aware of how these children can find changes and transitions difficult, scary and overwhelming. When we understand this, it can then inform our practice and help us to put in place strategies to support them.

Listening to children

For 15 years my work was focused on listening to children and their right to participation. I worked for a national children's charity, and we were commissioned by the local authority to support schools, nurseries, charities, social services and health services in how they listened to children and involved them in decision making. Through this work, I realized that one of the main areas children wanted to have a say in, wanted to be supported in, was managing change. I understood early on that with some of the biggest changes children encountered (e.g. moving school, being removed from home, changing foster placement, having medical treatment), they were not always supported as well as they could have been and this inevitably caused distress and sometimes led to very poor mental health. An underlying principle to our team's work was that children have a right to give their view and be listened to.

A key area that we were promoting was listening to children when they were encountering change, enabling them to have a voice about what they were experiencing and for adults to listen to this. Part of our team was involved in advocacy work with children in the care system, this was in the early 2000s. At that time, many charities were challenging social services over how children in the care system were being given black bin liners to contain their belongings when they moved to a new home; another issue was around the notice these children were being given. There were some stories of children coming home from school to be met by the social worker and told they were moving placements there and then, with no preparation.

Back in 2004, research was carried out by the Social Care Institute for Excellence, who were recommending that, wherever possible, children should be consulted, involved in the decision making and prepared for foster placement changes.[4] In 2018, the Children's Commissioner did some research, titled 'Voices of Children in Foster Care', with 100 children in the care system.[5] One of the findings from this was that the majority of children said they had met their new carers prior to moving, but had been given no information about the house, what it looked liked and other people in the household. One six-year-old child said they would like to see pictures of the house first. Reading this research saddened but did not surprise me: in my current job, I have worked with children who have been taken into care or who have had to move foster care homes, and I know that sometimes these children are still given very little preparation or warning.

In 2010, a research paper for the National Foundation for Educational Research was written on supporting children through transitions; its full and very long title is 'Ensuring that all children and young people make sustained progress and remain fully engaged through all transitions between key stages'.[6] Their recommendations included that practitioners should focus on the whole child and support young children to have the skills needed to cope with future transitions, and that good practice includes inductions and visits to new environments. Later on in this book, I am going to look at how we can do that practically.

When I was a child, children were rarely told about what was happening or informed about changes that were occurring.

---

4   www.scie.org.uk/publications/guides/guide07/placement/placement

5   www.childrenscommissioner.gov.uk/wp-content/uploads/2018/05/VOICE-OF-CHILDREN-AND-YOUNG-PEOPLE-IN-FOSTER-CARE.pdf

6   www.bl.uk/collection-items/ensuring-that-all-children-and-young-people-make-sustained-progress-and-remain-fully-engaged-through-all-transitions-between-key-stages

Thankfully, with huge changes in practice, we now know we need to prepare and support children through change. However, there are still many occasions when children report that they were not prepared enough, that they were not supported or that they didn't really understand what was happening. The next chapter is going to look at children's wellbeing and mental health, and how supporting children with transitions and change can support this. It will also consider how much information we should give to children.

References

Brodie, K. (2018) *Birth to Three: Holistic Development*. London: David Fulton.

Burke-Harris, N. (2018) *The Deepest Well: Healing the Long-term Effects of Childhood Adversity*. London: Bluebird.

Conkbayir, M. (2017) *Early Childhood and Neuroscience: Theory, Research and Implications for Practice*. London: Bloomsbury Academic.

Garvey, D. (2018) *Nurturing Personal, Social and Emotional Development in Early Childhood*. London: Jessica Kingsley Publishers.

Mainstone-Cotton, S. (2017) *Promoting Young Children's Emotional Health and Wellbeing: A Practical Guide for Professionals and Parents*. London: Jessica Kingsley Publishers.

O'Connor. A. (2018) *Understanding Transitions in the Early Years: Supporting Change Through Attachment and Resilience* (2nd edn). Abingdon: Routledge.

Sunderland, M. (2016) *What Every Parent Needs to Know: The Incredible Effects of Love, Nurture and Play on Your Child's Development*. London: Dorling Kindersley.

Chapter 2

Supporting Children's Wellbeing

For a long time there was a belief that you didn't need to tell children about what was going on. I sometimes still hear people of my parents' generation saying 'Of course, the children didn't know that there was something wrong.' We now know this is often unhelpful. Children know when things change; they pick up on the unspoken words, the change in the atmosphere, the body language.

I grew up with a mum with bipolar disorder. In the 1970s the main treatment was hospitalization, and my mum spent time in a psychiatric hospital on average two or three times a year through my childhood. I always knew when she was ill, or becoming ill. I used to warn my younger sister of the impending hospitalization. I did this before any adult told me it was happening. There were warning signs that I learnt from a young age. The main ones for my mum were spending more money and baking lots of cakes – this always then led to a crash of despair and depression. I just knew that my little sister needed to be warned that Mum would go to hospital again. Fortunately my dad had the insight to sit down and tell us each time she was going in, so we usually knew the day before the admission. I have spoken to other people who experienced similar childhoods, and they were sometimes never told what was happening, leaving them feeling very confused and scared. I know my early childhood experiences have been a huge catalyst for the work I do now, they have given me insight and understanding that has been so valuable.

Thankfully our understanding has developed since the 1970s and, as adults, we are better at preparing and supporting children with changes. However, I still hear comments from parents and grandparents who don't tell children about changes because they are worried it will cause them distress or that they are too young to understand. I recently heard of a family who replaced the pet rabbit for one that looked identical because they didn't want to upset the five-year-old with the idea of the rabbit dying. Or the family who knew the grandad was dying but they didn't tell the four-year-old he was poorly and in hospital as they didn't want to upset the child. Or another family who moved house but didn't tell the three-year-old and had them stay at Grandma's then arrive at the new house with no warning. Now in all these scenarios, clearly the parents felt they were doing the best thing for their child and didn't want to distress them or didn't think it would make much difference; however, in each situation the child did find out in the end and was distressed. I understand that many parents may struggle to know the words to use or how to support the child with changes; that is where early years practitioners are so useful – we can offer ideas and words to support the family, and help the child and parents at these times.

If we can help children deal with changes and loss from a young age, if we can support them, listen to them, guide them through it in a calm way, then we are giving them crucial life skills and supporting their wellbeing.

Filling in the gaps

One reason that adults are often worried about preparing children and telling them about changes comes out of a fear or anxiety about how the child will react. Or, when it is a very stressful situation for the adults, their own huge worries and fears and stresses can take over and they can find it hard to know how to support the child or which words to use. Nadine Burke Harris (2018) talks about how children need to make sense of what is happening to them – if we do not tell them, they will make up a story, they will fill in the gaps, and I know from my own work with children in the care system how this can happen. Because of this understanding, there is now a big emphasis on children who are in care still having contact with their birth families. Also, children who are adopted and long-term fostered now often have something called life story work, which enables them to have an understanding about what their story is, helping them to make sense of their story and give sense to what has happened. Jaqueline Wilson's (1991) children's book *The Story of Tracy Beaker* describes very well how a child can make stories in their head and fill in the gaps when they are not given the real information about what is happening. When we don't give children the real information and they fill in the gaps, this can cause long-term distress and confusion.

When to tell children

One of the big dilemmas for adults is around when we tell children something and how much information we give. There can never be an easy answer to these questions. It depends so much on the age, stage and developmental understanding of the child. As I was writing this chapter, I discovered a link to a parent's blog about telling a child he had autism.[1] It's a really interesting perspective, her child had the diagnosis of being on the autistic spectrum at the age of four, and she finally told him when he was eight. The mother didn't tell him at age four because she was concerned about how he would respond, and the often-negative views around autism caused her to feel fearful. Her reflection when she did tell him was that she should have told him sooner, and that with support it would have been helpful for him to know and he would have coped with

---

1   https://changedforgoodautism.blogspot.com/2017/04/the-day-my-son-learned-he-was-autistic.html

it. Winston's Wish, a national charity supporting children who have experienced bereavement, suggest that children are able to deal with truth, even very painful and sad truth, but so often as adults we underestimate this.[2]

I regularly hear adults say that the children don't know what is going on when there is something serious happening in the family; this is almost always a false understanding on the part of the adults. Children know when something is wrong, they may not know the details but they often sense the change in the adults, in the atmosphere. We may think we are good at hiding things, but often we are not and children pick up on small changes and realize something is wrong. The advice often shared from professionals who support children at times of great sadness (e.g. when a parent has cancer) is to give the amount of information that a child can deal with, dependent on their age and understanding. For example, with a young child you might say *'Daddy is poorly, he needs to be in hospital for the doctors to help him'*; for a slightly older child you might say *'Daddy has cancer, he is having some treatment in hospital, when he comes home he will be very tired for a bit.'* Later in the book I have chapters on serious illness, and death and bereavement.

Question for practice

Take a moment to think about your own experience as a child of being prepared or told about life-changing events. This can be painful to do, so be kind to yourself, but it can be helpful to think about how we responded when we heard about or experienced big changes in our early life. You might want to consider how you felt, how you were supported, how you were told.

---

2   www.winstonswish.org/serious-illness

Too much information

Sometimes, the other extreme can be parents giving children too much information that the child just cannot cope with. When we are talking to children about changes or difficult situations, we need to be mindful about how we are feeling and ensure that we are not projecting our own fears and adult worries onto a child. Children do need to know things, but they don't need to know everything. For example, I knew one mum who needed a hysterectomy, and she told her five-year-old that she was having a serious operation which would mean she would never have children again – the child would always be a single child. This was far too daunting and scary for the child, who needed to know that Mum was going to hospital for an operation on her tummy, that she would be in for a few days and then would need some rest when she came home; the child didn't need to know the mother's additional fears and upset. When we share information with children we need to ask a few key questions:

- How much do they need to know?

- How much will they understand?

- How am I feeling about telling the child this?

- What support will the child need and who can give it? (This may need to be from someone other than the parents.)

If you recognize that telling the child something difficult is raising lots of strong feelings in yourself, you could ask another trusted adult, one who is not so emotionally involved and charged, to support you in this conversation. I think it is important to remember that, as parents, we don't have to proceed with difficult conversations with children on our own, we can ask for help. Again, early years practitioners can perform a vital role in supporting parents in these conversations, offering support before, and often during, the conversation.

Too many transitions

In my first book, *Promoting Young Children's Emotional Health and Wellbeing* (Mainstone-Cotton 2017), I explore the idea of children's lives being very busy and often rushed. Even from a young age, our children can make many transitions and be involved in many different activities in a day. I do believe that we are at a time in society when it is all about doing: how many different things we do, how many different places we go to and people we see, how we fill our time. This is often also true in how we fill the time of children.

I suggest in the children's wellbeing book that we need to help children have times when they slow down, do less. Part of this is reducing the amount of transitions we expect children to experience. In early years practice there is now a growing move to having fewer transitions in a child's day. Anna Ephgrave is an advocate of this. In her book, *Planning in the Moment with Young Children* (2018), she gives an example of a timetable that is often found in Reception classes, a timetable full of stop-and-start moments – whole-class registration, assembly, literacy time, free-flow playing, snack time, playtime, maths, explore time, phonics, lunchtime, and this is just the morning! This is fairly typical of most of the Reception classes that I work in. Anna suggests there are other ways to structure the day; she has an alternative timetable she has used that has self-registration with free-flow play indoors and outdoors for 2 hours 15 minutes, whole-class phonics then lunch. Anna highlights how many children become stressed and anxious when they are experiencing lots of stops and starts. When they are in a flow moment of their play and learning and suddenly need to stop, they can find this very distressing.

Many of the children I work with in Reception classes really struggle with transitions, and I am always advocating for minimizing these. One school I worked in last year decided to try Anna's ideas: they had self-registration, they stopped the children going to assembly each day, they set up a rolling snack time, and they no longer went out with the whole school at play time but had free-flow indoor and outdoor play in their own class space. It was noticeable how much calmer and less stressed the children were. As well as enhancing their learning through highly engaged play opportunities, it was also clear to see that the children and staff were noticeably happier.

Ferre Laevers and his team at the Research Centre for Experiential Education at the University of Leuven in Belgium have developed a fantastic tool to help measure children's wellbeing and involvement. It is called the Leuven Involvement Scale.[3] This tool is very useful for helping us notice how good a child is at engaging in an activity, and how involved they are. This is a tool I have used many times; however, it is most useful when a child has extended time to engage, not just in a quick 15 minutes of free time on the carpet.

Question for practice

Take a moment to think about the timetable of the children you work with or your own children. How many transitions are there in the day? Then think about one or two children and reflect on how they cope with these transitions.

From this exercise a question to ask is, 'Do you need all those transitions?' If the answer is 'yes', then think about what is in place to support children so they don't feel stressed by the transitions. Consider how you prepare them and pre-warn them.

Moving up to the next room or class

One transition that many children experience is the moving of classes/groups and staff. It is common practice in the UK to move a child from the baby room to the toddler room and then pre-school room in nursery as they reach certain ages. Once in school, they

---

3   web.plymouth.gov.uk/documents-ldtoolkitleuven.pdf

often move class and teacher each year. I have observed on trips to Sweden and Denmark that their early years settings have a different practice: they have family groupings. A family grouping is where a child will enter the setting in a mixed-age group and then stay in that group, with those staff, through their years in the setting. There are a few nurseries that do this in the UK, but in my experience they are in the minority.

The family grouping is also common practice in Steiner kindergartens and schools. I really like the family grouping model, I think there is something very positive in having younger and older children together, learning from each other, helping one another. I also think it can be really positive for a child's wellbeing when they have the chance to build up a close relationship and attachment with a few members of staff who stay with them for a few years. In the UK, the time we most often see this model is with childminders and it is one reason why many families choose to have a childminder. When I have seen this practice implemented in nurseries in the UK, I have been impressed at the wellbeing of the children and how well the staff know and are able to support them.

We know that moving children frequently from one age room to another can cause huge stress for them. A friend of mine recently described to me how her 15-month-old granddaughter had changed rooms from the baby to the toddler room; she explained that before the move the little girl was walking, beginning to talk, confident and very happy to be in nursery. After the move, she stopped eating, became upset when her parents left her in the morning, slowed in her development of talking and went back to choosing to crawl instead of walking. This was clearly a very distressed and stressed 15-month-old who was confused at the change. These stressed behaviours lasted a few weeks. If she had been in a family grouping, that wouldn't have been necessary.

We also occasionally see this family grouping in schools, but mainly in small schools. My own children went to a small village primary school where they had mixed-age classes and would often have the same teacher and teaching assistants for two or sometimes three years. For my children, this worked really well – older children helped the younger children, the staff knew the children very well and the stress of moving classes and teachers was reduced throughout their school life. This way of working is sometimes called vertical grouping. There are now some senior schools in the city I live in who are using the vertical grouping idea for their tutor groups. They have found that vertical groupings have been beneficial to all ages and have created less tension between year groups. Anne O'Connor (2018) has some excellent information from practitioners, managers, children and parents about their experience of vertical grouping in early years settings and schools. In a later chapter I look at ideas of how we can support children in moving rooms/classes.

Holding children's wellbeing in mind

Our understanding of what influences and impacts children's wellbeing is growing continually. In the last three or four years, the wellbeing of children and adults has become a greater concern, and there are so many elements for us to think about and a growing number of great books on the subject. This is an area I have reflected on and considered thoroughly over the last few years, and one of my reflections has been that sometimes it can be the small, constant changes that have a great effect on some children.

We expect death, moving house, changing school to be a cause of stress for children; however, sometimes we overlook the impact that constant change within the day can have on a child's wellbeing. This is one reason why routine, clear communication and consistency is so important for young children – it helps them to feel safe. Often, when we see children becoming distressed and showing us their distress in challenging ways, this is their way of telling us they feel unsafe and unsure about what is happening. An important question for us always to ask when this occurs is, 'What is the child trying to tell me right now?' Keeping in mind the small transitions that can happen in a day, key questions to ask are:

- Does this transition need to happen now?

- If it does, how am preparing the child for the transition?

A constant conversation I have in schools and nurseries is around how we prepare children for the small transitions during a day. A few key ideas I try to implement are:

- Use a visual timetable to show the child what is happening – for a child who finds transitions very hard, use an individual visual timetable.

- Use Now and Next visual cards for individual children – *'Now we are having a snack.' 'Next we are playing.'*

- Always use a pre-warning before a change. Some settings use a bell to show that in five minutes it will be tidy-up time. With an individual child who finds this hard, pre-warn them, have their key person tell them individually and how them with Now and Next cards it will soon be...

- Use sand timers to show that an activity will be ending.

- Use emotion language to recognize how a child is feeling – *'I can see you are feeling very cross that we need to stop playing, when we have finished lunch we can go back to playing.'*

These are all small interventions, but they really support a child who is finding change overwhelming. They will help to ease the transitions and help them to feel calmer.

The rest of the book is broken down into change chapters. Each chapter will look at different changes and transitions that a child may experience in their life and will give practical ideas and suggestions on how you can support a child through them.

References

Burke-Harris, N. (2018) *The Deepest Well: Healing the Long-term Effects of Childhood Adversity*. London: Bluebird.

Ephgrave, A. (2018) *Planning in the Moment with Young Children: A Practical Guide for Early Years Practitioners and Parents*. Abingdon: Routledge.

Mainstone-Cotton, S. (2017) *Promoting Young Children's Emotional Health and Wellbeing: A Practical Guide for Professionals and Parents*. London: Jessica Kingsley Publishers.

O'Connor. A. (2018) *Understanding Transitions in the Early Years: Supporting Change Through Attachment and Resilience* (2nd edn). Abingdon: Routledge.

Wilson, J. (1991) *The Story of Tracy Beaker*. New York: Doubleday.

Practical Strategies

Chapter 3

New Siblings

New baby

For some children, this will be the biggest change they encounter in their young life – moving from being the centre of their parents' world to having suddenly to share that attention with a new person. This can sometimes be a painful and unpleasant shock. How older siblings respond to another child in the family can often be a big concern for parents. Parents often have many worries around how older children will react, whether they will be jealous, how they can support the child's strong feelings, how to deal with sleepless nights again (presuming the eldest child is sleeping, which of course is not always happening), how to manage a baby and an older child (or children).

As parents, we all hope that our older children will be lovely to their new sibling and that they grow up as good friends. This can happen; I am a parent of two girls (now 19 and 21), and my girls mostly had an excellent relationship and friendship as they were growing up, and still do, but this took a lot of intentional effort and planning, and the support of both me and my husband. Before we had our second child we talked a lot about how we would support Lily, our eldest, not to feel left out and how to help her when she had strong feelings of disliking her younger sister.

It is so important that we give thought and preparation to how we can support an older sibling, both as parents and as early years practitioners. Margot Sunderland (2016) describes how positive wellbeing in a child can be quickly lost when a new sibling arrives and can be quickly replaced by an overwhelming feeling of *my mummy loves my brother/sister more than me*. Initially there may be lots of excitement and positive feelings in the older sibling about the new arrival, but this will fade. We then need to be able to support the child with the new feelings. The rest of this chapter will offer some ideas of how to support the older child.

Preparing for the new baby

Some parents choose to tell children very early on in the pregnancy about the new baby. The decision of when to tell the older child will be different for every family and every child. It's important to remember that nine months is a long time to wait; as adults we can find the nine months long, but for young children this can feel like forever! Telling a very young child early on that you are having a baby will not make a lot of sense when there is a long wait. Many parents will wait until the first trimester has passed and the initial fear of miscarriage has moved on before telling their children. Also many wait for the 18- to 21-week scan, when they have a clearer idea of the health of the unborn baby. Having a scan photo can be really useful to show the older child – you can talk about how the baby is growing inside Mummy's tummy and talk about how it looks now. If a child is slightly older (three plus), you can talk over the weeks about how the tummy is growing as the baby inside is growing. Once parents have told the sibling there will be a new baby, it is really helpful if the parents also inform the education/care setting at the same time. The child will talk about it, and the key person/childminder is in an excellent position to support the child through this change.

Using books to explain pregnancy

I am a huge fan of using books to help children understand what is happening. A few books I would recommend for under-fives about pregnancy are:

- *There's a House Inside Mummy* by Giles Andreae and Vanessa Cabban.

- *Waiting for Baby* by Rachel Fuller.

- *What's Inside Your Tummy, Mummy?* by Abby Cocovini – this one talks through how the baby grows and develops each month.

- *A New Baby Arrives* by Nicola Barber – this is more of a fact book and talks about before and after the baby arrives.

I would recommend nurseries and childminders having books on this subject. As a setting, you will have many new siblings arriving over the years, so having books that you can look at about being an older sibling, a new baby arriving and what is happening can be very useful.

For older children (four plus) who are asking questions about how the baby got inside Mummy, I would recommend:

- *Let's Talk About Girls, Boys, Babies, Bodies, Families and Friends* by Robbie Harris.

- *Where Willy Went* by Nicholas Allen.

- *Mummy Laid an Egg* by Babette Cole.

Looking at photos

As the pregnancy develops it can be helpful to look at photos of the children when they were babies. This helps them become familiar with the idea of babies. I know nurseries who have done this activity when several mums were pregnant – they have encouraged the children to bring in baby photos, and staff have done this as well. At home, families can also do this, looking at the baby photos of everyone in the family. Looking at baby photos can then lead on to conversations about where they were born, where the baby will be born, who was at the birth and where the sibling will be when the birth happens.

Early years practitioners can support children with this information, and parents can tell the key person or childminder what their hopes are for the birth; for example, '*Mummy will be going to hospital and Lucy will be staying with Nanny.*' Nearer the time of the birth, the key person/childminder can also talk to the child about this, reminding the child and helping them to feel prepared.

Involving the sibling in preparation for the new baby

Involving the sibling in getting everything ready for the new baby can be a lovely way to help to help prepare the older child. Sometimes, it can be details such as which room the baby will sleep in, what the baby will sleep in, how the baby will be fed, etc., that can cause stress for the sibling. For example, it can be helpful for them to know before the birth if the baby is going to be sleeping in the parents' room, which may cause strong feelings in the child if they are sleeping in their own room and the baby is sleeping with the parents. Gently explaining this before the baby arrives can help them to feel prepared.

Similarly, it can be good to involve the sibling in finding clothes and toys for the new baby, which may be ones they wore or played with when they were a baby. Often, the older child enjoys playing with and exploring the baby clothes and toys (this can include much older children!). Before we had our second baby we got out the old toys and clothes a few weeks before she was born. Lily, our eldest daughter, enjoyed playing with the old baby toys for days on end; she also enjoyed dressing her dolls and bears in the baby clothes and by the time baby Summer had arrived, Lily had become bored again with the toys. This lowered her feelings of *'that is mine'* about the toys when the baby arrived. As early years practitioners, we can offer suggestions and guidance to parents about this.

Introducing baby dolls, nappies, feeding

Having toys available for children that include dolls, beds, blankets, nappies, bottles, carry slings, prams, etc., is often part of a continuous provision in early years settings and in many homes. These are particularly useful in helping a child to be prepared for a new baby. You can use the dolls to show a child how a baby is held, for example supporting their neck, how to change a nappy, how to be careful around the head, how to bath a baby and how the baby will be fed.

I would advise a childminder or key person to ask the parents how they are hoping to feed the baby and then talk to the child about it and include it in the play. For example, if you know they will be bottle feeding, include real baby bottles; if you know the mother will be breast feeding, talk openly about this to the children. Using play and toys is a very helpful way to assist children in feeling prepared for the new baby. Through play, you can explore feelings and anxiety the child may have. You can also model and talk about how to be gentle with a new baby, what they need and how to take care of them. I have also used a board game called New Baby Lotto, by Orchard Toys, which is another useful tool in talking about what babies need.

Using visual aids

As early years practitioners, we regularly use visuals to support children with special educational needs and English as an additional language. Visual timetables, for example, are now a feature in almost every early years setting. Visuals can also help children prepare for and understand changes. If you know a new baby is arriving, it can be a good idea to have a variety of photos – different babies, places that babies sleep, different ways of feeding a baby, different ways of transporting a baby, babies being changed, playing with babies. You could have these as a set of laminated photo cards that you make up and look at and use as a conversation tool; these could be used one to one or in a small group, or they could be used in an early years setting, in a childminder setting or at home.

Using books to understand how it will be when the baby arrives

Trying to explain to a child what it will be like when the new baby arrives can be difficult. They will understand the idea of a new baby, but they may think the baby will stay for a little bit and then go. As mentioned before, I always turn to books to help children understand about having a new baby. Some children find it easier to think about baby animals rather than baby people. There are a few books I would recommend, and as I was writing this part of the book I messaged some friends who recently had second babies to check which books they like. The list below is a selection of my own recommendations and those of recent parents and early years practitioners.

- *The New Baby* by Anna Civardi.

- *Let's Talk About My New Baby* by Stella Gurney and Fiona Freud – this has photos in it instead of illustrations.

- *My New Baby* by Rachel Fuller.

- *There's Going to Be a Baby* by John Burningham.

- *Spot's Baby Sister* by Eric Hill.

- *Aren't You Lucky!* by Laurence Anholt – this is one of the few books that addresses the subject of a child not feeling happy about the new baby and the strong negative feelings they have.

- *Mummy's Growing a Baby!* by Beth Thomas – this is a gentle book looking at the baby growing, the birth, where the baby sleeps and how it is fed.

What can the older child do?

One fear of parents can be that the older child will feel left out. During the transition to a new baby arriving, it is so important to talk openly about feelings and emotions. Having an emotional vocabulary helps a child understand what is going on for them; for example, helping them to understand that it is ok for them to feel cross at the new baby crying all the time, but it is not ok to hurt the baby.

Before the baby arrives, the parents and early years practitioners can talk about what the older child can do, and early years practitioners can offer useful support and guidance to parents on this. For many parents, this will be a new experience – an older child and new baby can be very daunting. The key person/childminder will know the child and is in a good position to offer thoughts and ideas. Some examples could be:

- Singing to the baby to help calm the baby. They can begin this before the baby arrives, singing to Mummy's tummy; the new baby will recognize the sibling's voice when it is born.

- Once the baby has arrived, sticking the tongue out and seeing the baby copy. This idea is from the book *The Social Baby* by Lynne Murray (2010). The baby will watch and copy, and this is joyful for everyone. You can explain to the older child that the baby loves watching faces and that they are helping to develop the baby's brain.

- Helping to bath the baby (with an adult's support).

- Rocking the pram.

- Helping to find nappies and choose clothes.

The key with this is follow the child's lead – if they want to be involved then enable it, with close supervision, but if they don't want to, don't force it.

Spending time with the older child

The big difference for the older child when the baby arrives is going from being the centre of their parents' attention to suddenly having to share it. Early years settings and parents may find that the older child becomes more clingy or aggressive, or possessive. These are, of course, normal behaviours. During the time of change the key person in the nursery or childminder can try to spend more one-to-one time with the child, giving them extra attention and giving them space to express how they are feeling. It can also be good if parents can spend some one-to-one time with the older sibling – keeping routines such as bedtime story and bath time are so important for the older child, and also having times with a parent when the baby is not around. If possible, get a grandparent or a friend to look after the baby while the parent and child spend some lovely time together, doing something they both enjoy – playing a game, being in the garden, reading a book. If the extra person can take the new baby out for a walk this can be even more special, giving the older child and parent some uninterrupted time together.

CASE EXAMPLE

In my nurture role, I worked with one four-year-old whose mum was having a baby and we knew that the baby would be going into the neonatal unit once born. For the weeks running up to the birth, all of my sessions with the girl were based around play with babies: each week I took in a toy baby, a cot, blanket, nappies and baby clothes. I found out from the mum how the baby would be fed and then took in a bottle and baby milk. Through play, we were able to explore how the baby would be cared for, where she would sleep, who would feed her and how she would be fed.

As we knew the baby was going into the neonatal unit, I also took in photos of the local unit, and we talked about the doctors and nurses that would be looking after the baby, how Mummy would be staying in with the baby for a few days and then the baby would stay on her own for a bit. We discussed who would be looking after the little girl while Mummy and baby were in hospital and how she would be able to visit them. I also used the game New Baby Lotto by Orchard Toys – this was a favourite game of the girl and we played it each week. It was another useful tool for talking about all the different things the baby needed and what she could do to help when the baby arrived.

Supporting siblings if the unborn baby dies

Sometimes, a pregnancy will end with a miscarriage or the later death of an unborn baby. This is such a difficult time for the parents; as well as having their own huge emotions, they will also need to support their children in understanding what has happened.[1] Early years practitioners can support the family and child through this, offering stability and routine to the child and support to the parents. The sibling may have many questions about the death and why it has happened. It is important to answer the questions honestly but also simply, explaining that the baby was not growing and was not able to live outside Mummy's tummy and has died. Be guided by the child's questions and reactions, showing them that it is ok to feel sad and

---

1   For some useful suggestions on how to tell siblings about the death of an unborn baby, see www.babycentre.co.uk/a1014794/explaining-a-pregnancy-loss-to-your-child

you are there to love and support them, and that it is ok to talk about it if they want to.

Adoption and blended families

For most families, a new sibling arriving will be through the mum being pregnant; but for others, it will be through adoption. Many of the ideas above will be relevant for this, and having an open and honest conversation with your child/ren is vital. The adoption process in the UK is not a quick one, and the parents will be guided through it by a social worker, part of whose role is to consider the needs of their children. CoramBAAF adoption and fostering[2] are able to offer guidance to families who are adopting and fostering. They have a produced a useful booklet for children, suitable for around five years plus, called *Adopting a Brother or Sister* (Argent 2006).

The arrival of new siblings can also be though blended families. This is happening far more today, and children still need preparation for this. A useful book to explore how all families are different is *The Great Big Book of Families* (Hoffman and Asquith 2011). The key to having new children arrive in the family, whether they are through birth, fostering, adoption or joining of families, is talking to, explaining and listening to the children, remembering to involve them in the conversations and the preparation.

The arrival of new siblings can be the biggest and most exciting, as well as sometimes daunting, transition that many children will experience. However, with the right support and care from parents and early years practitioners it can be a positive experience.

---

2   https://corambaaf.org.uk

References

Allan, N (2006) *Where Willy Went.* London: Red Fox.

Andreae, G. and Cabban, V. (2001) *There's a House Inside Mummy.* London: Orchard Books.

Anholt, L. (2015) *Aren't You Lucky!* London: Red Fox.

Argent, H. (2010) *Adopting a Brother or Sister.* London: CoramBAAF.

Barber, N. (2009) *A New Baby Arrives.* New York, NY: The Rosen Publishing Group.

Burningham, J. (2010) *There's Going to Be a Baby.* London: Walker Books.

Civardi, A. (2005) *The New Baby.* London: Usborne.

Cocovini, A. (2007) *What's Inside Your Tummy, Mummy?* London: Red Fox.

Cole, B. (1995) *Mummy Laid an Egg.* London: Red Fox.

Fuller, R. (2009) *My New Baby.* Swindon: Child's Play.

Fuller, R. (2009) *Waiting for Baby.* Swindon: Child's Play.

Gurney, S. and Freud, F. (2013) *Let's Talk About... My New Baby.* London: Campbell Books.

Harris, R. (2007) *Let's Talk About Girls, Boys, Babies, Bodies, Families and Friends.* London: Walker Books.

Hill, E. (2012) *Spot's Baby Sister.* London: Puffin.

Hofffman, M. and Asquith, R. (2011) *The Great Big Book of Families.* London: Frances Lincoln Books.

Murray, L. (2010) *The Social Baby.* London: CP Publishing.

Sunderland, M. (2016) *What Every Parent Needs to Know: The Incredible Effects of Love, Nurture and Play on Your Child's Development.* London: Dorling Kindersley.

Thomas, B. (2014) *Mummy's Growing a Baby!* Transition Story Books.

Chapter 4

New Pets

The benefits of pets

Pets bring many benefits to a family or early years setting; children can learn so much through having a pet they help to care for and be gentle with. However, I have worked with an increasing number of children who have found the introduction of a new pet to the family home very stressful, so this is the reason for writing this chapter. As adults, we can often presume that the introduction of a new animal will be straightforward and does not need preparation, but I have learnt this is not always the experience of families.

Introducing animals into the home or early years setting can be an excellent way to help children adapt to a change. Having animals in the home or setting is also useful for helping children learn about taking care of others, and being kind and gentle. They can also, as some families and settings realize, be a gentle way for children to learn about death; for example, fish and gerbils, which have a shortish lifespan. Animals can have a calming effect on children too, and there is interesting research around autistic children finding dogs therapeutic and enabling them to access more of the world around them.[1] A growing number of schools now have dogs visiting for children to read to them,[2] and I know of several schools, both

---

1   www.supportdogs.org.uk/blog/willow-the-wonder-dog-makes-normal-life-possible-for-youngster-sam
2   https://petsastherapy.org/what-we-do/read2dogs

mainstream and special needs, where teachers or the head teacher bring their dog into school. Every time I have observed this, the calming impact the dog has on the children and the staff is visible.

As a family, we have always had pet guinea pigs; our children have experienced so much joy from the guinea pigs, and the guinea pigs have also been a comfort to the girls at times when they fell out with friends or were finding school hard. Both of my girls have some sensory-processing challenges, and the guinea pigs were very calming and grounding for times when they felt a bit overwhelmed. Over the years, there have been many deaths of the guinea pigs (guinea pigs only live for around six years), but this has been helpful for us to speak honestly about death and the difficult feelings that surround the subject. Both my girls are now at university, and they have both said they wished their guinea pigs could go with them!

Preparing for a new pet

If you are going to introduce an animal into the home or early years setting it is a good idea to prepare children before you do this. Here are some ideas on how you could do this.

Images and discussion

Talk to the child about the new animal you are going to get. If you have already decided on what type of animal, then show them images (e.g. photos of dogs, cats or rabbits). If you have not decided on the animal, you could involve the children in a conversation about different animals and look at a range of pictures, thinking about the size, where they would live, how much exercise they would need, how much food they would eat, etc. It is worth doing some research first – the Blue Cross charity has some useful fact sheets on different animals and their needs.[3]

---

3   www.bluecross.org.uk/pet-advice/choosing-right-small-pet

Visit to a pet shop or rehoming charity

Before you bring the pet into the home or setting it can be a good idea to go and visit animals in either a pet shop or a rehoming charity. I know a nursery that arranged a visit to the local pet shop when they were considering buying guinea pigs. Staff from the shop showed the children the different animals and talked to them about the care needs of the animals, including the type of home the guinea pigs would need, and what they can and cannot eat. The children were able to ask questions, and the nursery staff were able to see how the children reacted to the animals.

Toys to practise taking care

Once you know what type of animal you are getting, you could buy some toys to use to practise looking after the pet. You can buy most toy soft animals now (e.g. hamsters as well as dogs, cats, rabbits and lizards!). With these you can practise using kind hands, petting not pulling, patting not hitting, stroking not pulling. You can also use the toys to talk about the food they will eat and where they will sleep, how and when to pick them up (always with adults) and what equipment they will need (e.g. feeding bowls, leads, water bottles).

Information about looking after your pet

There is a lot of information available about children and pets. Make sure you have done your research first – children will potentially be upset if you talk about getting a dog but then discover you cannot afford it and have a mouse instead! The RSPCA website has pages with information about children and dogs, how to choose the right dog and how to help children and dogs to both be safe.[4] The Blue Cross website has useful information about children and puppies.[5]

---

4   www.rspca.org.uk/adviceandwelfare/pets/dogs/company/children
5   www.bluecross.org.uk/pet-advice/puppies-and-children

The Cats Protection organization has information about cats and children.[6] If you know parents are thinking about getting a dog or cat, it is worth signposting them to these websites, and there is a useful article on daynurseries.co.uk website about a variety of nurseries that have pets and how the children have benefited from them.[7] You will, of course, need a policy for this.

Books for children

Throughout this section I am recommending using books to help children learn and understand more about changes that are happening. There are many excellent books for children about looking after animals, and there is also a useful website called pets education, which has a range of fact sheets and activity ideas for early years children on how to look after pets.[8] Usborne have a wide range of pet guidebooks about looking after pets, and I would also recommend having books about being kind to pets. One little boy I am working with at the moment has been very rough with his pets at home; we have been using books to talk about kind hands and being gentle; and we have also been using toys to practise being kind to the animals.

The references list that follows comprises books that I particularly like on pets and looking after animals.

References

Child, L. (2008) *I Completely Know About Guinea Pigs.* London: Puffin.
Harris, R. (2004) *Goodbye Mousie.* New York, NY: Aladdin Paperbacks. [A book about death of an animal]

---

6   www.cats.org.uk/help-and-advice/cats-and-children
7   www.daynurseries.co.uk/news/article.cfm/id/1558044/from-cute-and-fluffy-to-slimy-and-wriggly-how-pre-schoolers-care-for-day-nursery-pets
8   www.peteducationresources.co.uk/learning-resources/for-teachers/early-years

Howell, L. (2013) *Looking After Guinea Pigs* (Usborne Pet Guides). London: Usborne.

Miller, V. (1999) *Be Gentle!* London: Walker Books.

Starke, K. (2013) *Looking After Dogs and Puppies* (Usborne Pet Guides). London: Usborne.

Verdick, E. (2005) *Tails Are Not for Pulling*. Minneapolis, MN: Free Spirit.

Yolen, J. and Teague, M. (2010) *How Do Dinosaurs Love Their Cats?* New York, NY: Scholastic.

Chapter 5

Going on Holiday

The idea of going on holiday will often excite children, but for some children it is a change that makes them feel anxious, unhappy and sometimes afraid. We know this can particularly be relevant for children with autism, but it can also affect other children as well. As we have been exploring, children can find any change overwhelming, and taking a holiday can become a stressful experience. In this chapter you will find ideas that parents and early years settings can to use to help prepare children for a holiday and hopefully alleviate some of the stress around this.

Preparing for the holiday
Telling the child
If you have a child who finds change challenging, always think carefully about how to prepare them for a holiday. If early years settings and parents work on this together, they can help the child to feel less anxious. Early years settings can advise parents about things they can do to help the child feel less worried.

A few weeks before the holiday, start to talk about going on holiday. You want to give the child some time to prepare, but not too much. Remembering days and weeks are hard for children to understand, and for some children too much anticipation can be equally stressful, so this needs judging carefully according to the individual needs of the child.

You could have a calendar to mark off the sleeps before they go on holiday. Parents could print out pictures of the place they will be staying in or explore a website with the child looking at different images of the location. If the early years setting knows where the family is going, the key person can also look at this with the child, spending some time over a few days before the trip looking at the images and talking about what will be there and what they might see.

Here are some things to consider to tell the child:

- the place you will be staying (e.g. hotel, caravan, tent, house)

- how you are going to get there (e.g. car, rail, air, boat)

- where they will be sleeping (e.g. in the same room as you, in a bunkbed, with siblings)

- who is going

- what types of things they will do (e.g. going to the beach, walking in woods, swimming or a visiting a theme park).

And don't forget to remind them that they will come back to their home and nursery afterwards.

The journey

If the journey to the holiday destination is on transport other than your car, this is an extra area to consider. Mumsnet has a really useful article with tips and ideas on how to travel with children, looking at rail, boat, car and air travel.[1] There are now many advice pages on the internet specifically about air travel with young children. One I

---

1   www.mumsnet.com/travel/how-to-survive-journeys-with-children

particularly like is by the netdoctor, which has advice from Dr Margot Sunderland.[2] There are also a few YouTube videos that explain to children what happens in an airport around security. All these changes can be scary for children, but if we can explain to children before the experience then this goes some way to help prepare them. One of the clips I like is from the US Transport Security Administration (TSA) – an animation showing how to go through airport security.[3] Wizz has a YouTube video with a child talking about being on a plane – it describes the noise and what you can do on a plane.[4]

For children with autism, there is now a growing recognition by airports of the need to provide extra support. Shannon Airport in Ireland and London Gatwick Airport (North Terminal) both have free-to-use sensory rooms for people with autism, cognitive impairment, dementia and other special needs. Passengers can book a 45-minute slot in this room at the special assistance desk. This recognition is beginning to grow across the world, with more airports beginning to follow the lead of Shannon and Gatwick. London Heathrow Airport has also introduced the sunflower lanyard scheme, which recognizes that not all disabilities are visible; the lanyard enables staff to see that you have a disability and they are able to offer additional assistance if you need it.[5] Parents may not know that this kind of assistance is available, but early years staff are in an excellent position to let families know about the help they may be able to receive.

Play about holidays

Offering children play opportunities about going on holiday is an excellent way to help to prepare them. This needs careful

2   www.netdoctor.co.uk/parenting/baby-and-toddler/a26277/tips-for-childs-first-flight

3   www.youtube.com/watch?v=IHjlN5lzCjM

4   www.youtube.com/watch?v=AFIJfX_5tvE

5   www.heathrow.com/airport-guide/assistance-at-heathrow/hidden-disab ilities?fbclid=IwAR07060y13EcpfLjT-3mgsZDwhwzyHXrHVSueTw7K-VF n2pcOZ59jU6Lh44

consideration. I have been in some settings (often Reception classes) where they turn the role-play corner into a travel agency. I have always found this idea very strange, but particularly now – how many children go to a travel agent? And how does a travel agent link with going on holiday for a four-year-old? Most holidays are now booked online, so having brochures of foreign destinations is an outdated idea and not at all relevant for children.

An alternative idea is to bring in resources that link to holidays, e.g. suitcases and things you might need on a holiday. This could include sunglasses, beach shoes, swimming costume, towels, buckets, spades, suntan lotion, sun hat, teddy bear, etc. Or, if it is a winter holiday, it will include winter clothes. Staff could have conversations with the children about what they think they need on a holiday.

If you know children are having a holiday in a caravan, campervan or tent, make sure you have some relevant toys to play with. Sylvanian Families® have a toy caravan, Lego® and Playmobil® have a campervan model, Playmobil® also have a good range of camping toys, which include tents and camping gear. You could set up a small pop-up tent in your setting, with sleeping bag, air bed, small stove (don't include the gas!), plates and cups. This would give the children the opportunity to try these out, play with them and explore them in the safety of their early years setting or at home. If you know the travel will involve air, rail or boat, provide toy aeroplanes, trains or boats for children to explore and play with. The key person should be available to support this play and answer any questions.

Books for children about holidays

There are a few books I would recommend for adults to read to children about holidays as preparation. Having a range of these books in the early years setting would be useful to call on when you know a child is going on holiday and maybe you could also recommend or lend them to families. The references list at the end of this chapter includes books that I particularly like.

Doing without a holiday
Remembering not all families are able to go on holiday

There are many families that early years practitioners work with who will not be going on holiday, or if they do holiday it may be a rare event. We need to be very aware of and sensitive to this. In settings that are term time, we need to think carefully about talking about what children did in the holidays, not presuming they have all gone away. Many of the children I work with do not take holidays, and if they do it is never to foreign countries, but is more likely to be camping locally or visiting family.

When we arrive back from half-term breaks or Easter holidays I will often ask the children I work with what they enjoyed doing in the school holiday. I might ask them if they went to the park or on a journey, or if there was a favourite toy or game they played with over the holiday. This opens up the conversations about the many varied experiences they may have had, giving value to all their experiences. If I work with a family where I know positive experiences are very limited in the family home, I might ask what was their favourite food that they ate in the holidays, or did they watch something on the TV or iPad that made them laugh. These are simple but important ways to connect with a child and their experiences outside of the early years setting, giving value to their world.

In the new proposal for Ofsted's inspection framework for early years, they are proposing to look at 'cultural capital'. There is much controversy around this. Helen Moylet wrote an excellent guest blog for Early Education, reminding us that cultural capital should not just be about middle-class aspirations and assumptions for children's experiences (e.g. whether they have visited the theatre or been on a holiday to a beach or a city break).[6] Her argument is that, as early years practitioners, we also need to recognize the value children bring when their cultural experience over the holidays has been going on the bus to visit their Granny who lives in the next city, or visiting the park and finding sticks and dandelions. We need to be mindful of the wide variety of cultural experiences that our children will have and celebrate this diverse mix.

Supporting children who are not going on holiday

As early years practitioners, as well as giving thought and attention to children who are going away we also need to be mindful of the children remaining in the nursery. Children may feel sad that their friend is away. At circle time you could talk about where the missing child is and wonder what they might be doing. You could ask the family to send a postcard to the setting so that you can share this with their friends. Some settings use a soft toy (e.g. a teddy bear) that goes on holidays with children, and the family are encouraged to take a photo of the bear and the child on their holiday to share with their friends when they return.

When staff go on holiday

Staff will be taking time off during the year, and this can be upsetting and unsettling for some children. When you know you are having time off, tell the children a few days before. If you are going away or doing something different, you could tell the children about this and show them a picture. Tell the children you will miss them and remind them that you will be back. If possible, send the children a postcard while you are away and maybe bring the setting a little something on your return (e.g. a beautiful shell you found or a picture of where you have been). While you are away, the setting

6   https://early-education.org.uk/news/guest-blog-helen-moylett-ofsted%E2 %80%99s-thinking-cultural-capital-some-concerns-and-questions

could have a countdown of days until you are back, helping the children to understand you are returning.

Day trips

Some settings, particularly Reception classes in school, will occasionally do day trips with their children. The idea of a day trip is lovely, often it offers children a different cultural experience, and I believe so much rich learning can take place outside of the classroom or nursery. However, some children can find these day trips very unsettling and can become very anxious.

Many of the children I work with find the big change in routine of such a day trip totally overwhelming. I am always amazed at how staff can forget that these children will need a lot of additional preparation. Below is a list of ideas to help support an anxious child in preparing for a day trip. These can be used with the whole group, benefiting everyone.

- One week before the trip, mention to the group where you are going.

- Over that week, show pictures of the place you are going to; this might be pictures of the things you will see, the building, the things you will do.

- Over the week, talk about how you will be travelling on the trip and what you will be eating (e.g. packed lunch).

- The day before the trip, remind everyone again about where you are going, how you are travelling, what you will be eating and who is going.

With the individual child who is anxious, as well as doing the above with the whole group, also have the key person spend some one-to-one time over the week going back over the arrangements. Talk to the child about who they will sit with on the journey and which person they will be with during the day. Talk to them about their feelings around this and give them a chance to tell you if anything is frightening them or if they are really looking forward to any specific part.

Supporting families

For many families, the idea of a holiday can be a mix of excitement and long anticipation, but sometimes the planning and preparation can be stressful. We often have so much invested in the idea of a perfect holiday, but unfortunately holidaying with children does not always bring the long-awaited rest and relaxation that adults may have experienced on holidays before children! Early years practitioners are often in a position where they offer ideas and thoughts to parents about what makes holidays a little less stressful, for example preparing the children, thinking and preparing for the journey, thinking about food the child likes to eat and maybe taking that with them, thinking about a few key toys the child likes to play with and taking those for the times the family are not out and about and doing things.

References

Civardi, A. (2005) *Usborne First Experiences: Going on a Plane*. London: Usborne.

Cousins, L. (2005) *Maisy Goes Camping*. London: Walker Books.

Cousins, L. (2011) *Maisy Goes on Holiday*. London: Walker Books.

Cousins, L. (2016) *Maisy Goes by Plane*. London: Walker Books.

Smith, S. (2015) *Usborne First Sticker Book: Airports*. London: Usborne.

Chapter 6

Moving Home

Some children will experience moving house rarely, and when they do it will be a carefully planned and organized event by the adults in their lives. Other children may experience moving home many times in their lives, and this can be under stressful circumstances such as eviction and homelessness. Some children may experience a sudden move without notice, particularly if there is domestic violence in the home or violence/danger in their geographic area and the family need to go to a place of a safety. Or families such as Travellers and Gypsies may regularly move location, taking their home with them.

Early years practitioners need to be aware of how to support children and families through different home and location moves. Whatever type of move it is, the experience of moving home can be stressful for all involved. Even when it is a planned and wanted move, the experience of finding a new home, packing, moving all belongings and unpacking can be a trying and stressful time for the adults; and the children will often pick up on this stress. This chapter will explore different ways to help children with home moves, offering ideas for parents and for early years practitioners in how they can support the child.

Planned moves

When families are moving house and this is planned, it can be both exciting and stressful. We know that there is so much involved, from finding the new property, sorting and packing and organizing, and then the actual move. Adults may feel excited and be looking forward to the move, but this can be a very confusing and frightening experience for children. As I have mentioned in earlier chapters, the key is giving children the right amount of information, support and notice.

One of the problems with moving house is that the timing does not always work as planned, especially if you are buying a house, and this can make it tricky to help keep the children informed. Children need to know about the move; some children will need a lot of notice and lots of opportunity to talk through this change; other children will manage with shorter notice. This is about knowing the needs of the individual child. But in all moves, where possible, children need some time to prepare. Early years workers are in a good position to support the child and family in this.

How to prepare children

If possible, visit the new house as a family before the move, taking photos of the house, rooms and garden if there is one. If the house is in a new geographic area, the family could also visit the local park and shops, taking photos of the new area. Photos can be looked at as a family, and the early years setting could ask the family for the photos so that the key worker can also look at these with the child and talk about the move.

Talk to the child about how the family will move; for example, whether they will be using the family car with friends and family helping or hiring a removal company. Explain how everything will be put into boxes and taken from the old house to the new house. The key worker can build on this information, talking to and reassuring the child that their toys, bed, pets, and so on, will move with them.

If possible, involve the child in some of the preparation. You could, for example, get the child their own box to pack some of their things in. You could also talk about their new room, and, if the family are able to redecorate, talk to the child about this and involve them in some of the decision making (e.g. colours of paint, carpet or curtains).

If the child is older and verbal, give them space to ask questions. They may want to know why they are moving; they may ask whether their friends and family will see them at the new house or if their toys are moving with them. The child may ask questions or comment about the move while they are in their education setting; staff can answer questions and let parents know the questions that are being asked.

The night before the move, remind the child what is happening and how it will happen (e.g. *'We will have breakfast, and then we are going to put all the boxes in a big van to go to the new house'*). Some families choose to have their child in nursery or with family/friends when the actual move happens. If this choice is made, it is important to make sure the child knows that when they leave, they are saying goodbye to the house and then will be saying hello to the new house. Give the child space to do this – saying goodbye to the house may make them feel sad, and that is ok – having chance to say goodbye is an important part of moving on. It is important to acknowledge the emotions the child is feeling; you could say *'It's ok to feel sad at saying goodbye to our old house.'*

Play around moving house

When early years settings know a child is moving house, they could introduce some big boxes and parcel tape into their provision, and talk about packing things up and moving them – other children and staff could share their experience of moving. Early years staff need to give the children space to explore through play: packing boxes, moving things around, making marks on the boxes, going in and out of the boxes, etc.

Early years practitioners can encourage the parents to allow the child to play with some of the boxes at home, and there could be a few boxes set aside for them child to play with. They may want to explore being in and out of the box; they may want to pack it and unpack it. I would have this available for the week or two running up to the move, to give the child space to explore the idea and experience through play.

Once the move has happened, it is worth keeping some boxes for a little while for the child to continue to play and explore the idea of moving.

Books about moving house

I recommend that the early years setting has books about moving house and, where possible, lends these to the family or recommends that the family borrows them from a library. As I have mentioned in previous chapters, children's books are a great way to help us explore a change with children. Through the story we can talk about feelings and emotions about the change; through exploring change with a story the child is also supported to ask questions and think about the change that is happening. Some of the ones I like are:

- *The Big day! Moving House* by Nicola Barber – this is not a story but more of fact book, it talks through the different elements to moving day and feelings around this.

- *Usborne First Experiences: Moving House* by Anna Civardi.

- *A Little Princess Story: I Want to Go Home!* by Tony Ross.

- *Moving Molly* by Shirley Hughes.

Sudden moves

Some families need to move suddenly. This year, I have worked with a refugee child whose family has experienced several moves and another family that moved very suddenly into a refuge, because of domestic violence, and then into a new home. Both of these children experienced moves under stressful circumstances. At times of crisis like this the family are rarely able to prepare the child. It is so important that early years staff are able to support the child and family at these times.

With a refugee child, early years practitioners need to seek guidance and support. Support is available for refugee families and early years settings working with them, and it is important that early years workers link in to support systems. If there is an early years team in your local authority, they will be able to offer some advice on how to support the child and family and which teams in your area are able to help with this. Some areas have refugee support teachers who will come into the setting and offer advice; other areas have teams set up to support the families and practitioners working with the family. The National Association for Language Development in the Curriculum has an advice sheet for supporting refugee children in the early years foundation stage.[1] *Nursery World* had an article in 2001 about supporting refugee/ asylum-seeking children,[2] and although this is a dated article the tips are still relevant. Islington Council has a refugee and asylum seeker support pack for early years practitioners.[3] The common thread in these articles and packs is that early years practitioners need to seek advice from agencies that specialize in support work with refugee families, to be welcoming, supportive to the families,

1   www.naldic.org.uk/eal-teaching-and-learning/outline-guidance/ealrefugee/ refey

2   www.nurseryworld.co.uk/nursery-world/news/1087833/asylum-seekers-children-country

3   www.islingtoncs.org/system/files/Supporting%20refugee%20children%20 in%20the%20early%20years%20pack.pdf

to have translators available to support with language needs and to give children space to play and explore their feeling and emotions.

Supporting refugee families is a specialized area. A colleague, Donna Gaywood, who works as a children's centre teacher, is researching refugee children's everyday experience of early education for her PhD with the Centre for Research in Early Childhood. Below, she offers some ideas from her research.

Refugee children and early education – Donna Gaywood

It is important for staff to remember that there is no such thing as a *typical* refugee child. All the children and families who have been awarded refugee status have probably had an average life in the country they have come from, before they were forced to flee. It may be that a child in your setting is not yet recognized as a refugee, so their family could be seeking asylum. This involves trying to prove to the authorities that their lives would be in danger if they returned to their own country. The asylum-seeking process is often very difficult, and the uncertainty can cause very young children significant stress.

So, it is important to remember that refugee children can be managing several significant challenges when they come to an early years setting, which extend far beyond the obvious language barrier and the migration journey.

The family may be experiencing hostility, overt racism or unconscious bias, which can lead to deep feelings of isolation. There are likely to be cultural differences, which can mean that the children and their family may not understand the 'unspoken rules' of the setting. Refugees have also often had to leave all that is familiar, including friends and close relatives. The children may be experiencing trauma or profound grief and may not know if their loved ones are safe. The parents and/or siblings may be experiencing mental health difficulties, and this can impact how the children feel and cope in nursery.

Here are some top tips which could help:

Your attitude is all important

How you interact with the children's families and the children themselves will be far more important than what you do or say. People who find themselves displaced are very sensitive to unspoken vibes. They will know if you are sincere, even when there is a language barrier. Parents are often very concerned about their children and are keen for them to make friends and achieve. Try not to think of refugee children as essentially vulnerable. In reality, refugee children often have high levels of resilience and a strong inner core.

Allow yourselves times to reflect

There is a lot to think about when you are supporting refugee children and getting to know their families in an early education setting. It is important to allow and enable staff to spend time together to reflect, setting up purposeful staff meetings for this. Migration and refugees are an emotive subject. Many people have strong views. Practitioners could feel worried, afraid or inadequate, given the circumstances the children may have experienced. It is important to talk through these feelings in a positive atmosphere. Staff need time to reflect on their own unconscious biases and discuss any issues or incidents that have occurred.

Be proactive making relationships with parents

Forming a positive relationship with refugee parents is very important for the children in your setting. This can be tricky for a number of reasons. Trust is a key element. Refugee families may have experienced extreme circumstances and might be wary of people who are in authority. Try to be sensitive to the power balances in the relationship and aim to offer welcome and dignity to them. Parents often prefer not to be defined as 'refugees' and may not like this as a label for their children. Be persistent and committed to developing this relationship.

Develop difference and diversity provision

Find out about the refugee children's language, culture and customs. Don't be afraid of the language barrier and not understanding the cultural differences. It is important to be open with the parents and admit if a mistake is made. The children live in two different worlds and they adapt very quickly. To help them feel secure and thrive, it is important to provide a bridge between their two lives. Having a good ongoing celebration of difference and diversity, which goes beyond tokenism, will do just that. Spending time developing this will be very beneficial.

Support children to belong

Helping displaced children to feel like they belong will speed up their language acquisition and help them to begin to make friends. They need to feel welcomed, and it is likely the incumbent children will need to be shown how to do this. Developing a peer buddy system and having small-group times will help. Increase their sense of self and belonging by having small, named activity groups (e.g. butterflies, ants, etc., with their own labelled area). Having photographic name cards for mealtimes alongside a strong key person approach will also be beneficial.

Regular, clear routines and boundaries will support a refugee child, as they will learn how to predict what comes next. Offering visual support for every activity will also help. Operating defined and clear 'golden rules' that are taught regularly will support children to feel safe and help them settle. Making friends is one of the most important factors in assisting the children to regain their equilibrium. Try not to assume that making friends will happen naturally for refugee children. As a setting, intentionally plan to support the children to make friends. Offer them turn-taking games with other children, lead and follow games and circle songs.

Be responsive

Displaced children are ordinary children who are likely to have experienced extraordinary events. It is unrealistic to assume that they will always respond as other children might when they are in your setting. It is likely that you will have to change what you do and how you do it, to best support the child. Ensure that you are responsive to the child and their family, feeling confident to try new approaches to enable the child to feel safe, to access early education and to make friends and flourish.

Family violence or homelessness

Children who have experienced sudden moves due to domestic violence or homelessness may have moved into a refuge, safe accommodation or temporary accommodation. These families will often have a social worker involved, particularly if domestic violence a factor. Early years settings should seek advice from the social worker on how to support the family and child. Women's Aid has a useful document about how the child who has moved into a refuge may be feeling and how they may behave.[4] Most of us will have no experience of living in a refuge and it may feel overwhelming supporting a child or family in this position. The charity Refuge has an information sheet about living in a refuge,[5] which I think is a useful read for early years staff.

---

4   www.womensaid.org.uk/information-support/what-is-domestic-abuse/
    impact-on-children-and-young-people
5   www.refuge.org.uk/our-work/our-services/refuges/living-in-a-refuge

Living in temporary accommodation

Some children we work with may be living in temporary accommodation due to homelessness, and sometimes this happens very quickly. Early years workers can seek advice from health visitors, and children's centre workers will also be able to offer support. I know that currently in the UK there is a massive cutback in children's centres, so if you are unsure about your local connections, contact your early years team in the local authority for advice, or your local health visitor team. If you are concerned about the welfare of the family contact your local social services team. The charity Shelter has a useful guidance sheet on supporting homeless children.[6]

A friend of mine, Debbie Harvey, works for a homeless charity in Bristol supporting families. She offers some ideas on how to support a family who are experiencing homelessness.

Supporting homeless families – Debbie Harvey

Becoming homeless always comes as a shock for families, even if they know it's coming. Parents often try to hide it from their children, but they pick up on the anxiety. It is really important to prepare the children, but also to reassure them. Children often think being homeless means sleeping on the street, but parents and workers can reassure them that in the UK children don't have to sleep on the street. However, in many places, especially in London and other large cities, homeless families can end up living in temporary accommodation. This is often cramped and small, and families may not be allowed to take their furniture or many belongings with them. I always suggest that before the day of leaving they give each a child a box, a large shoebox or similar, and the children can fill this box with the most precious thing

---

6   https://england.shelter.org.uk/__data/assets/pdf_file/0007/263248/Children_and_family_services.pdf

they want to take with them. Parents can then make sure that the box stays with them wherever they go. I also tell parents to take their own bedding with them to temporary accommodation because having your own duvet cover and pillow makes the accommodation feel more like home.

I recommend to parents that they try to get out every day with their children while in temporary accommodation because often there is no garden and little room to play. A visit to the library, a city farm, a park will be beneficial to the whole family. I remind families they will always be rehoused eventually, but not to put their lives on hold while they are waiting. I also suggest that parents try to be positive with their children and make the temporary accommodation as much like home as possible. Little things like having some flowers or a nice cushion can help make it feel more homely. If parents feel their child is becoming anxious or depressed, then they need to see the GP.

Resources

I have found it very difficult to find books for children about being homeless or living in temporary accommodation. I think this is an area that could benefit from stories being written for children. On the area of refugees and asylum children, I feel this is such a sensitive area that I would be reluctant to recommend a book on this. There are a few children's books; however, each child who has arrived here has had very different experiences, and I haven't yet found a book that can address all of these sensitively and appropriately for younger children.

Compassionate staff

In all these situations, it is so important that the children know they are safe and welcome and that they belong in their early years setting. They need staff who are compassionate and nurturing, paying particular attention to the child's wellbeing. The play opportunities in their early years setting will be particularly important to these children, as they may have very limited play opportunities in the home; the early years setting needs to be an emotionally rich and supportive environment for them.

Homes that move

Some of the families you work with may be Traveller or Gypsy or Bargee families (families who live on boats and barges). Some of these families will move regularly, although this is becoming a lot harder, with people being regularly moved on and fewer places to move on to. Other Traveller and Gypsy families will live in a van/caravan/vehicle on a fixed site and move less frequently.

The team I used to work for worked with Traveller and Gypsy families in Somerset, Bath and Dorset for over 20 years. For the last two of these years, I managed this work and we had a tiny playbus that we took onto sites. Over this time we developed ideas and resources to use with the children. For early years settings that have Traveller and Gypsy families it is important for staff to have an understanding about Gypsy and Traveller needs and lives, including the differences between the communities.

A charity called Friends Families and Travellers has a useful website[7] and publications with information, and The Traveller movement also has a useful website.[8] Most local authorities used to have a Traveller and Gypsy education support team (or person) and were able to offer advice and support to education settings about how to best support the families. Tragically, many of the posts and teams have been lost due to local authority cutbacks. However, if you have Traveller children in your setting, it is worth enquiring whether there is a Traveller education support team or person.

I always recommend that when early years settings have Traveller and Gypsy families in their area they have toys and books available

---

7   www.gypsy-traveller.org
8   www.travellermovement.org.uk

that represent different types of homes. We are often very good in early years settings at making sure we represent families from other countries and languages, but the Traveller and Gypsy communities are often not represented through books and toys in schools and nurseries. Some of the toys I would recommend are toy caravans, white vans, horse trailers, buses, barges – all these are examples of different homes that some families live in. You can buy all of these for not very much expense from toyshops or online.

Many of the local authority Traveller and Gypsy education teams used to make their own resources that they sold locally or online; sadly lots of these resources appear to have disappeared with the teams, but it is worth googling or looking on auction sites for resources – you may find some second-hand. Some of the books and resources I have are:

- Specialized children's puzzles from Durham Ethnic Minority and Traveller Achievement Service – these have pictures of caravans and traditional Gypsy vardo wagons.

- *Mikela's Black Beauty Goes to School* by Dirk Walker and Julia Worth.

- *Mikela at Home* by Dirk Walker and Julia Worth.

- *Shaun's Wellies* from the Norfolk Traveller Education Service.

- Tess the Traveller series by Fiona Earle and Ross Huelin – a series of ten books for and about Travellers.[9]

Foster care or adoption

Some of the children we work with will be moving into a foster home or a new adoptive family. Within early years, the aim is, where possible, to have children adopted and to minimize the number of

---

9   www.gypsy-traveller.org/pdfs/tessorderform.pdf

foster homes a child has, but this is not always achievable. I have worked with children who have had numerous foster placements in a short space of time. As I mentioned in Chapter 1, the best practice is to give the children information and preparation for this move, although this does not always happen.

I recently worked closely with a social services team, virtual school, foster carers and a nursery on a change for a four-year-old child, which involved a large geographic move. Some of the things we put into place were showing the girl before the move:

- photos of the new house, including bedroom, garden, toys

- photos of the new family, including pets

- photos of the area – a significant piece of information in this situation was that the new family lived near a beach.

The photos were shown to the child when she was first informed by the social worker and before the first meeting with the new carers. The day after she was told of the move and shown the photos, she made a visit to the new home, and then a few days later, the new carers visited her in the foster home.

Once the child was settled in the new family home, life story work was being carried out by a social worker, with photos and descriptions of families and homes she had lived with. This will be a life story book about her, which she will keep and, where necessary, it will be added to.

The nursery that she was moving on to had information about the specific activities she enjoyed (e.g. sensory play), and they ensured they had these for her to play with when she arrived. One of the things I regularly did with the little girl was to give her a hand massage with hand cream that I always had with me. She found this activity very calming and asked for it every time she saw me. I shared this information with the new setting and they bought the brand of hand cream that I used, so the smell would be the same and familiar. We know that the sense of smell is an important sense for children and can help them to feel they belong. By the nursery purchasing the same hand cream and using this, they were providing something that was familiar and safe to her.

There are many ways early years practitioners can support children and families through a home move. Staff need to be curious about how the child is feeling, how the move is affecting them and what further support they may need. We need to remember that, as early years practitioners, we are in a privileged position to help the child and family.

References

Barber, N. (2008) *The Big Day! Moving House.* London: Wayland.

Civardi, A. (2005) *Usborne First Experiences: Moving House.* London: Usborne.

Hughes, S. (1991) *Moving Molly.* London: Red Fox.

Ross, T. (2009) *A Little Princess Story: I Want to Go Home.* London: Anderson Press.

Norfolk Traveller Education Service (1995) *Shaun's Wellies.* Norwich: Norfolk Traveller Education Service.

Walker, D. and Worth, J. (2007) *Mikela's Black Beauty Goes to School.* Bristol: Avon Consortium Traveller Education Service.

Walker, D. and Worth, J. (2007) *Mikela at Home.* Bristol: Avon Consortium Traveller Education Service.

Chapter 7

Starting School or Nursery

When we think about children's transitions, the main area we often consider is a child starting school or nursery. We know that this is a major change in a child's life and one that we need to give a lot of thought to and make preparation for. I think that within early years settings we have become a lot better at supporting children and families through this. There are many fantastic books for professionals about how to support children in the transition to school, one I particularly like is Tamsin Grimmer's book *School Readiness and the Characteristics of Effective Learning* (2018). Tamsin unpicks the idea of 'school readiness' and promotes the idea of schools being child ready, and how, as parents and early years practitioners, we can support the child.

This chapter is going to outline some practical ways we can help a child in the transition and some ways the school or nursery can be ready for the child. I work as a nurture consultant supporting four-year-olds in their transition to school, the four-year-olds I support have been identified as having social, emotional and mental health difficulties. Transition to school is a huge focus for most of my working week. This chapter will share some of the ideas and tools I and my colleagues use.

Preparing the way
Beginning to talk to the child about school/nursery

In the few months leading up to a child starting school or nursery, it is important for the adults around them to talk about this change. Doing this in a gentle way, such as when they drive past the school or nursery commenting on it, for example *'That is going to be your school/nursery.'* I always suggest that parents avoid using the words *'when you are a big girl'*, as this is very confusing for children and can add additional stress, I have heard some children reply to this *'I am not a big girl'* or *'I don't want to be a big boy.'* Instead they could say *'When you are four you will go to school.'* Once parents know which school their child is going to, and this is known by April, it is a good idea for them to start regularly noticing the school with the child as they drive past or walk past. They could say things such as *'Oh look! The children are outside playing today – when you go to school you will be able to play outside as well.'*

Supporting parents

As early years practitioners, we need to remember that some of the parents we work with are feeling hugely anxious about their child starting nursery or school, and, in my experience, particularly starting school. This is especially true if the parent has not had a positive experience of school themselves or if they are fearful that their child has some additional needs, which may make the entry to school harder. It is so important that early years settings support parents through this, starting with reminding them about the time to register their child for school, not just reminding once but gently checking in with them that they have registered their child. Then talk to the parents about which schools they are choosing and recommend that they visit the schools. I know nurseries who tell parents about the local schools' open days, and remind parents in their newsletters and emails about the registration day.

In supervision and team meetings I recommend that a discussion is had about the children/families you are particularly concerned about and, as a team, plan how you are going to give them extra support in reminding them to fill in the registration form. Sometimes early years workers don't think it is their role to encourage parents with this; however, I would really encourage every early years worker to see it as their role. If a family does not register their child and this gets picked up late, it can be very late in the term before that child and family know where they are going, which makes the transition process very stressful for the child, the family and the receiving school.

Home visits

I am a big fan of home visits, and I encourage all the schools and early settings I work with to do these. We introduced home visits when I was Chair of Governors at my children's school and found them so helpful, both for the families and the staff. I know that home visits take time, but I think this is valuable time to put aside. A home visit can help a child and family feel more at ease – it gives the parents time to have a conversation with the staff in their home environment, and it enables the staff to see the family and child in their familiar environment.

I always advocate having two members of staff for a home visit, partly as this is good safeguarding practice but also because it allows one member of staff to talk to the parents and one to play with the child. This is often a time when essential forms, such as medical forms, can be taken to the family, and paperwork about the setting can be left for them. More importantly, this is also the time to find out about the child: what they enjoy playing with, how mealtimes are and what they like to eat, what their sleep routine is, whether they have a comfort toy or a transitional object they use, whether the child has any particular fears or things they find difficult.

Tait and Prodger (2017) from the Pen Green Centre[1] talk about the home visit as a great opportunity to start building a trusting relationship with the family and find out information about the family and extended family that is relevant to the child. An example they give is finding out who looks after the child and any shift work patterns parents may have. Many of their children are cared for by parents and extended family, with shift work being a common feature for them, and knowing and understanding this helps the staff in their planning. All children attending Pen Green have an allocated family worker who will do at least three home visits a year. Penn Green advocate this and find that their 'integrated collaborative approach to working with families really helps support the child' (Tait and Prodger 2017, p.47).

Having discovered what the child likes and enjoys, the staff can hold this is in mind when they are planning for the child's first visit. I have found that many children are delighted that their new staff have seen them at home and will often talk about it when they start at the new setting. I know settings that bring a home visit book giving information about the setting, and leave it with the family. Some settings do one for parents with written information about policies, fees, times, etc., then another one for the child with pictures about the nursery (see below for more details about this).

Planning the settling-in process

For a child who is starting at nursery/pre-school or with a childminder, the setting should have a well-planned settling-in process, which should involve several play visits to the setting with a parent. Ideally, there will have been a home visit where the key person has found out important information about the child and has used this information as part of the settling-in plan for them.

---

1   www.pengreen.org

A friend, Wendy Baker, who used to be a manager of a nursery in London, introduced an 'all-about-me' kit for new children who arrived. The key person would make an all-about-me kit about themselves, and they would then share this with the new child and parent on their first visit or at the home visit. The kit told the family something about the key person, who would then encourage the families to do one for the child to bring with them on their next visit. I have taken this idea and I use it when I meet the new children I work with. I have a small bag with a wind-up swimmer, a shell, a photo of my family, some bubbles, a pressed and laminated flower from my garden and a small lavender soft pillow. All these items represent different things about me, what I love and the work I do. I love this idea as it helps in early communication and relationship building with the child.

It is so important to give focus and attention to how we support a child to settle and transition into the new setting. This may take time, however; but if we get it right, it makes life so much easier for child, parent and adults in the setting. Below is an example from a friend called Louisa Tickner of how she supports babies in this transition in her role as a childminder

Supporting babies in transition to a childminder – Louisa Tickner

Our settling-in processes are not prescriptive and are very much child- and family-led. The length of the settling-in period is determined by a number of factors from information gathered at the very early stages of meeting a family. My approach to gathering information is:

- I want to know whether the baby has been left with other people. And if so, how frequently and with whom.

- If this is the family's first baby, I am aware that there may be an anxious mum/dad that needs just as much

settling in as the baby does. As a childminder, I need
to consider the parents' needs; for example, they may
not want to go back to work but have to for financial
reasons, and therefore they may be feeling quite
bereft about the thought of leaving their baby with
someone else.

- I find out whether the baby/child was born at full term
(very tactfully of course), and whether they spent time in
hospital.

- Is the baby currently breastfed? Does the baby co-sleep?
Is the baby breastfed to sleep for both daytime naps
and bedtime?

- I find out about comforters that the baby may have.

Once I have gathered all the information I need to plan for
settling-in, I start off gently. I know from experience that getting
the settling-in period right it will make everyone's lives much
more relaxed. I also need to consider the needs of the children
already at the setting and how an unsettled baby will effect them,
the needs of the parents who may have to leave an unsettled
child in my care, which can be very hard for a parent to do, and
my own needs of managing and coping with an unsettled child
all day.

I usually try to have three visits a week if I can, two as a
minimum. The visit times need to be when the baby/child
is fresh, so not just before a meal or nap time – we want the
times of settling-in to be associated with feeling happy, relaxed
and content. I start off with just an hour's play with baby and
parent and build that up. If the baby is not clingy to the parent or
constantly looking for them, I will encourage the parent to sit a bit
further away and engage the baby in play, enabling the baby to
move between myself and the parent. Mealtimes are then built
into the settling-in time; for example, the parent and baby staying

for lunch together with all of us. Daytime naps are built in last, with the parent usually settling the baby to sleep themselves. I generally ask them to pop home while the baby sleeps and I get them up and see how long they can manage a play before the parent is called back.

For breastfed, co-sleeping babies, I usually find we just have to work together to build up the daytime naps in a cot once the child starts properly. This is often a progression of being rocked off to sleep in a buggy close to where we are, then the buggy going in the room they will sleep in, and then progression to the cot – no one is left to cry themselves to sleep. If you are working solo, this will need to be adapted to work with the other children in your care. I always ask for babies that are still breastfed for mum to sleep in a t-shirt and then pop it in the change bag the next day and I use this as a comforter for the baby; it works so well. I also ask for the baby's cot sheet to come with the baby for the first couple of weeks; familiar comforting smells offer so much reassurance. If the baby goes to sleep with the t-shirt, I make sure it is well wrapped up in a ball so the baby can't get themselves tangled in it.

The whole settling-in period can run to anything from two to six weeks, but depending on baby and parents an average length of time is two to three weeks. Between myself and the parents, we gauge at what point they will start leaving them for short periods of time. There will inevitably be those placements where unfortunately there can't be much settling-in time.

Flexibility through the transition process

I believe there needs to be flexibility where possible when a child starts an early years setting and school. We know some children find the settling process much easier than others. At Pen Green Centre they have a two-week settling-in process, where the parent or another adult carer, such as a grandparent, is with the child to settle them. The carer is able to spend time in the nursery room with the child, and also move into another room for a drink and some short time away from the child, while still being on the premises. The staff find this gives parents an opportunity to learn and see how the centre works; it also enables staff to get to know the families. I know other settings that have children in for short visits with parents and then visits where the child does a shorter stay on their own. As we all know, some children will settle well and quickly, but other children will find the settling process very hard and it will take them longer. I understand it can be complicated with the variety of hours that children do and fitting in with parents' jobs; however, I know from experience that if we recognize that every child is going to have different needs in the transition, having a flexible approach is more supportive of the child's wellbeing.

I am also a big advocate of a staggered transition into the start of school. In the city I live in, schools have many varied transitions into the setting – some schools do a week of half a day, a week of half a day with lunch, and then, in week three, children are in full-time; other schools do a variation on this, but I also work with a few schools who have adopted the straight in, full-time from day one, process. One argument in favour of the full-time option is that children now attend nursery full-time, and most parents work and dislike the staggered hours. My argument is that the transition to school is very big, it is stressful for everyone and full-time in nursery is not the same as full-time in school. Even with the best early years play-based classes, the children still find the move to school huge. Schools are bigger, there are more children, the timetable is different, the expectations are different. I cannot emphasis enough, this is a big change for little children. In my experience the children who settle best, with the least amount of anxiety and stress, are those who have some staggered start to school. I know that parents and some head teachers often hate it, but our focus needs to be the best interest of the child. A head teacher I know said to parents that when children start school we are getting children to start something they have no control over, something they will be doing for the next 14 years of their life. For me, this really emphasizes why we cannot rush this start, if we can get it right at the start of their school life, if we can help them to feel secure, welcomed and safe, then we are setting a firm foundation for them to hopefully go on and thrive. This should not be rushed.

One exception for this is where a school has a foundation unit with the nursery and reception class together, in those set-ups, where the child has already spent a year in that setting/foundation unit, that makes more sense to be full-time from day one in Reception, as it is not a new experience.

School readiness or child readiness?

Having children school ready is a popular and commonly used phrase, particularly by government ministers. I personally really dislike the term 'school readiness'. As we all know, the Reception class should still be following the early years foundation stage – it should still be a play-based environment, all year. The term 'school readiness' implies that we are making children more ready for formal learning. Tamsin Grimmer (2018) unpicks this argument and encourages early years practitioners to speak out against this and to remember that 'school readiness is not about academic skills' (p.19). The Professional Association for Childcare and Early Years have suggested that 97 per cent of childcare and early years professionals agreed on a definition of school readiness.[2] This includes children who:

- have strong social skills

- can cope emotionally with being separated from their parents

- are relatively independent in their own personal care

---

2   www.pacey.org.uk/Pacey/media/Website-files/school%20ready/School-Ready-Report.pdf

- have a curiosity about the world and a desire to learn.

I love this definition, and these are the factors I work with. I believe that, as early years practitioners, a large part of our focus needs to be on supporting the child with the above skills.

Children who need additional support going into school

Some of our children will need additional support as they go into school. The children my team and I work with have been identified as needing extra support in their transition and into the Reception year. If we plan our transitions well for all our children, the children with additional needs will of course benefit from this. However, if you know you have a child in your setting with additional needs, they will need extra support. They may have a disability, they may have social, emotional and mental health needs, they may be a looked after or adopted child, they may be a summer-born baby or they may have been a premature baby. These children may have an Education Health Care plan, but not necessarily. As an early years setting, you have responsibility for ensuring that these children get additional support in the transition process. It is not just enough to inform the school of their additional needs, it is vital that you put in place some additional support for the individual child. Some examples of ways you could do this are:

- extra visits to the new school. I know early years settings that arrange a few extra visits to the school with the individual child. Sometimes this is for the key person and child, or it may be for two members staff and three or four children. This does take some organizing and it can be tricky for staffing, but it is so beneficial for the child

- extra time with the key person and child talking about school, talking about the change, looking at photos of the school and teacher, finding out how the child feels and whether they have any questions

- making sure the child has a photo book or video about the new school (see examples below)

- making sure the receiving school has good information about the child – if possible meeting the teacher, teaching assistant and SENCO to share key information about the child, what they enjoy, what they struggle with, what approaches work.

I also know a few nurseries who have released the key person for a few hours a day to go to school with the child in the first few days. This is offering additional support for the child in their transition. School, family and nursery all found this worked well.

I encourage schools to think very carefully about the hours a child with additional needs does when they start school. Most of the children I work with will have an extended transition process into the start of the school year, and this may mean they are still doing half days until half-term or Christmas. In some cases, I have children who have been on a reduced timetable for the whole of the Reception year. This takes some negotiating with the school and family, but I have found it is better for a child to have a good three hours in school where they cope, they are happy and they are beginning to adapt to being in school, than having a child in school for six hours being miserable, violent, disruptive and distressed.

Activities and resources to aid transition
Play and conversation around going to school

In the term running up to the start of school (from June to September), I recommend that nurseries start to introduce more items to prompt conversations about school. Here are some suggestions:

- a variety of school uniforms to try on, wear, play in

- school book bags to play with

- PE kits to try on

- photos of the schools the children are going to

- books about starting school (see suggestions below).

As early years practitioners, be mindful about talking to children regularly about going to school. This does not need to be in a formalized, circle time way, but, during the day, mentioning school; for example, commenting aloud, *'Lucy I know you love playing with the water, we must tell your new teacher when she visits how much you love water play, she will really want to know that. Your new teacher is going to be called...'.*

Photo journeys to inform new staff

A piece of work our team do with all the children we support is a photo journey booklet. The idea behind this is influenced by the Clark and Moss (2001) mosaic approach.

Get the children to take photos of what makes them happy in nursery, it can be a good idea to limit this to eight to ten pictures. Or, if children want to take lots when you make the booklet, get the child to choose eight to ten photos. Explain that you will use these pictures to show their new teacher/key person what they like and enjoy doing.

Ask the children about the photos and why they chose the images, and write up their words. Print the photos and words and make them into a small booklet. Pass the booklet on to the new school or new classroom, explaining to the staff that this is what the child enjoys in nursery or in their current class and these are the photos they wanted to share. I also send a copy home.

This exercise is very simple, it allows the new staff to see and hear a little about what the child enjoys and can help them in their preparation to welcome the new child.

In term five I do these with all my Reception children as part of their transition into Year 1. As I am writing this, I have just completed a week of photo journeys with my current case load, and every year I do this I am reminded of how these photos journeys enable us to see the child's world through their eyes. They are a very simple but powerful way of letting us see and hear what is important for the child. It may not be possible to do this with every child who is moving up to the new room or school; however, if you have children that you know will particularly struggle with the transition, then I would recommend that you give these children additional support and this is one tool you can use to do this.

By doing the photo journeys in term five or at beginning of term six, we are starting to gently help the children to think about the move ahead. Of course, the photos the children take on that day may not be what they still like in September, but often I find the children take photos that are themed. For example, most of my children this year took photos of the outdoor space. For all the children I support being outside is the thing they love most, even if the activities they do change, the overall experience of being outside is very important to them, and this is unlikely to change in September. This gives vital information to the new teacher, showing how these children need to have chance to be outside regularly. As a key person to a child, the early years practitioner will have this information and can tell the teacher, but when the teacher has documentation showing them this from the child, it is even more powerful.

Consultation story books

In my book *Listening to Young Children in Early Years Settings* (2019) I describe using consultation story books as a tool for hearing children's thoughts and feelings. I first used this tool when I was working on project for my undergraduate dissertation, which was linked with a transition project I was delivering with my local authority. For this project I worked with a small group of children to find out what they thought about school, what their worries and concerns were, and how much they knew about school. I created a simple story tool about a girl called Lily, who was starting school. The story told the children about what Lily would wear, which school she was going to, what she would do at lunchtimes, who her teacher would be and which friends were in her class. It also talked about what she was excited about and what scared her. Each page had a statement about Lily going to school, with an appropriate picture and a question for the child.

Examples of questions from the school story

Lily is going to her new school, it is called Camerton Primary. Where are you going to school?

Lily's school jumper is blue. What colour will your school jumper be?

Lily is going to school with her friend Megan. Which friends are going to your new school?

Lily will be going to school on the bike with her dad. How will you get to school?

Lily will be having school lunches at school. She likes eating jacket potato, What will you do at lunchtime?

Lily is looking forward to playing with the pirate boat in the classroom. What are you looking forward to at school?

Lily is a little bit worried about playtimes, the playground has a big climbing frame and she is a bit scared about that. Does anything worry you about school?

This is a very simple tool to design and use – it enables staff or parents to have conversations with the child about the school they are going to and how they are feeling about it. In a nursery or pre-school, I would recommend using it as a key person with a small group, giving the children the opportunity to talk about the different questions. This will give insight to the staff about how much the child knows and will enable staff to fill in the gaps, and go back and check with the family.

When I first used this tool I discovered that one of the girls in my group did not have the school uniform (this was just a few weeks before term started) and that she didn't know what she would be doing for lunch or how she would get to school. This highlighted to staff that they needed some conversations and to offer Mum some additional support around the transition. It transpired that Mum was feeling very anxious about the move and had not felt able to talk about it to her daughter or the staff.

A booklet about nursery or school

One of the ideas I suggested earlier in this chapter is a booklet about nursery or school. This is a really lovely project to do with your current children in preparation for the new children. Children have the best ideas about what new children need to know about school. The way to do this is:

- Explain to the children your idea.

- Ask the children what the new children need to know about the room/setting.

- Get the children to take photos in the setting, and, together, look at these and ask the children about them and why they are important.

- Put the photos and children's words into a booklet. Pass on the booklet to every new child.

This activity enables staff to hear what is important to the children and helps new children transition. I have used this many times and it has given me insight into how the children see their world. I once discovered how some children were initially frightened by the noise the toilet cistern made in the school, and this enabled us to give thought to this when the new children arrived.

Visits

Whether the child is starting nursery or school, there should always be visits before the date of starting. Many schools now have several visits booked for the class in the summer term before starting, also nursery and childminders will often organize visits to the setting before the starting date, enabling the family and child to look around and spend time seeing and experiencing the space.

I cannot emphasize enough how important transition visits are for the child's wellbeing. I know some schools who minimize the number of visits to the class as there is not enough time to fit many in. In my experience, some of the best practice is where the school and early years setting work hard together to plan visits carefully. I know one school and feeder nurseries who planned picnics together (including in the summer holiday) and 'stay and play' visits, the teacher or teaching assistants visited the nurseries two or three times and they also organized song time activities.

You may also have a child in nursery who you know is going to need extra support in their transition. With these children you could ask the teacher if it's possible for the child and parent to do an additional visit as mentioned above. This could be at the end of the school day, giving the child a chance to really explore the new classroom on their own. I had one nursery who, with the agreement of the school, filmed the child and the classroom at the end of the school day; they made a little video tour of the classroom and outdoor play space, and the child then took this home and was able to look at it regularly with his carer. This made such a positive difference to his transition.

Books for children

As I have mentioned throughout this book, using stories with children is an excellent way to help them with change. Having a range of books about going to school is a lovely way to support the child and helps with conversations. I suggest to nurseries that they send a list of books that families might like to borrow from the library about starting school or starting nursery. Below is a list of books that I like:

- *Going to Nursery* by Laurence Anholt.

- Maisy Goes to Nursery by Lucy Cousins.

- *Starting School* by Janet and Allan Ahlberg.

- *Usborne First Experiences: Going to School* by Anna Civardi.

- *Tom and Sofia Start School* by Henrietta Barkow – this is available as a dual language book in several languages.

- *The Big Day! First Day at School* by Nicola Barber.

The start of school or nursery is a big change for children, if we can help them manage this change with the least amount of stress and anxiety for them, we are making a great contribution to their wellbeing and helping them to have the best start in their long education experience.

References

Ahlberg, J. and Ahlberg, A. (2013) *Starting School*. London: Puffin.
Anholt, L. (2015) *Going to Nursery*. London: Orchard Books.
Barber, N. (2008) *The Big Day! First Day at School*. London: Wayland.
Barkow, H. (2006) *Tom and Sofia Start School*. London: Mantra Lingua.

Civardi, A. (2005) *Usborne First Experiences: Going to School.* London: Usborne.

Clark, A. and Moss, P. (2001) *Listening to Young Children: The Mosaic Approach.* London: National Children's Bureau.

Cousins, L. (2010) *Maisy Goes to Nursery.* London: Walker Books.

Grimmer, T. (2018) *School Readiness and the Characteristics of Effective Learning.* London: Jessica Kingsley Publishers.

Mainstone-Cotton, S. (2019) *Listening to Young Children in Early Years Settings: A Practical Guide.* London: Jessica Kingsley Publishers.

Tait, C. and Prodger, A. (2017) 'The Many Different Ways We Involve Families.' In M. Whalley and Pen Green Centre Team, *Involving Parents in Their Children's Learning: A Knowledge-Sharing Approach* (3rd edn). London: Sage.

Chapter 8

Family Changes and Separation

When parents separate

Going through a separation or divorce is often an extremely stressful experience for the whole family. All children will respond differently, but often they will experience this as a loss. The role of the early years practitioner can be so important to the child and family at this time. Often, as early years practitioners, we may feel that this is a private issue for the family; however, when we are the key person to the child in the education setting, we can be the consistent adult who remains calm and who doesn't have the emotional turmoil that the parents are experiencing. Early years practitioners are also in a position to offer some suggestions to the family.

Young Minds have a useful advice sheet on their website about supporting children through separation and divorce.[1] A few of the tips they give, which can be shared with families are:

- Listen to the child's worries and concerns and give them space to express their emotions and show that these feelings are ok.

---

1   https://youngminds.org.uk/find-help/for-parents/parents-guide-to-support-a-z/parents-guide-to-support-divorce-or-separation

- Give children honest information in a way they will understand.

- Provide reassurance – let them know it is ok to feel sad and it is ok to cry.

- Do not ask the child to take sides.

- Shield children from conflict between the parents – this can be frightening and make them anxious.

Children's behaviour changing

It is not uncommon for parents to be surprised at how calm younger children are in response to being told their parents are separating. This can be the initial response and it is often because young children have no concept about what separation or divorce means. However, as the weeks progress and the change happens, families may begin to see some changes in the child.

We know that children's behaviour is one of the key ways they communicate their feelings. If a child is experiencing a family breakdown, this will almost certainly change their behaviour. They may start sleeping less well, they may become upset when parents leave them at the nursery/childminders or school, and they may become violent or aggressive. These are all ways in which the child is communicating that they are scared, overwhelmed, anxious, confused and angry. They may not have the words to express this verbally, but they are still communicating their strong feelings.

Children need adults who are able to tune in, support them, make sense of the confusion around them, listen to them and reassure them. Once again, early years practitioners are in a vital position to help the child with these strong feelings and to offer them reassurance. The early years practitioner can also offer support to the parents in understanding any changes in the child's behaviour. While all feels chaotic around the child at home, they need to know that the early years setting is consistent, safe and nurturing for them. If you have a child in your setting who is experiencing these changes, it is very important that you discuss in supervision how to support the child and family and to think carefully about the familiar routine and environment you can provide for the child.

Providing clear information to the child

As I have discussed in every chapter, children need clear information about the change that is taking place. Parents need to ensure that the information they give to the child is enough to help them understand what is happening without giving them too much information and confusing them. This might be explaining that one parent is going to be living in a different house, or that the children are moving to a different house with one parent.

At a highly stressful time of separation, parents also need to ensure that they are keeping their own feelings and worries in check – it is never appropriate to criticize the other parent in front of the child. There are various websites available, offering suggestions about how parents can support children. The ones I recommend are Gingerbread,[2] Family Lives[3] and Relate.[4] The key messages from all of these are:

- The child needs to know it is not their fault.

- The child needs to know they are loved by both parents.

- The child needs to know what will happen (e.g. where they will live and with whom, how often they will see the other parent).

- The child needs to know they can talk to you.

---

2   www.gingerbread.org.uk/information/separating/support-for-your-child
3   www.familylives.org.uk/advice/divorce-and-separation
4   www.relate.org.uk/relationship-help/help-separation-and-divorce/dealing-childrens-feelings-and-behaviour

- Where possible, stick to the child's normal routine (e.g. bedtime routine, going to nursery, swimming lessons, play dates with friends).

- The biggest cause of negative impact on children is where there is conflict between partners and where a child cannot see one parent.

Voice in the Middle[5] have messages from teenagers based on their experience in childhood and teen years of finding out about their parents separation. Their top tips include:

- Tell the child that they will still see members of the family (e.g. the other parent, grandparents, stepchildren).

- Tell the child both parents still love them and always will.

- Make sure they know it is not their fault.

- Listen to the child, and to their thoughts and worries.

- Be honest and clear.

- Do not talk negatively about the partner.

- Do not coach your child to take sides.

Support the early years setting can give

Cath Hunter has written a piece on the Teach Early Years website titled Coping with Divorce, where she suggests that early years practitioners are in an important position to support the parents and the child.[6] She recommends:

- Practitioners need to respond positively to both parents; it is essential to not take sides.

---

5   www.voicesinthemiddle.com/for-parents/conversation/top-things-to-do-and-dont

6   www.teachearlyyears.com/a-unique-child/view/coping-with-divorce

- Have clear communication with the family about who is collecting and which home the child is going to. You can then remind the child on the day which parent they are going with, and you could use photos of the parent to show the child.

- Have clear communication with both parents about how the child is.

Louisa, the childminder who shared her practice in Chapter 7, told me how she made a picture diary of the week for a child in her care. This child lived half the week in the dad's house and half the week in the mum's house. The picture diary helped the child know which house he was going to and who was collecting him, and it supported him through the change.

Consistency for the child

When a child is experiencing a big change, such as parents' separation, the education setting can provide stability, consistency and calmness that they may not be experiencing at home. When settings know that a child is going through family separation, this should be discussed in supervision, giving careful thought to the additional support that the child may need. Where possible, try to make sure the daily routine stays the same in the education setting, with the same adults supporting them. If there are going to be changes in the routine or with staff (e.g. staff going on holiday), ensure the child is given additional notice and support around this.

It is important to remember that when a child is experiencing a significant change, other small changes that would normally seem insignificant may have a big effect on them, and their ability to cope with usual differences is likely to be lowered. I worked with a child who appeared to be coping with the family separation until a weekly routine changed slightly in nursery, and music session was changed to a gym session; at this change he became very distressed and really struggled to manage; that change became the tipping point for him.

Books and resources

There is a growing range of children's books based on the subject of parents and separation. Family breakup will potentially affect many of the children we work with, and because of this all education settings should have books for children on the subject. Early years settings are then in a position to recommend or lend the books to families. Some of the ones I particularly like are:

- *My Family's Changing* by Pat Thomas.

- *Two Homes* by Claire Masurel.

- *Dinosaurs Divorce: A Guide for Changing Families* by Laurie Krasny Brown and Marc Brown.

- *Two of Everything* by Babette Cole.

Parents in prison

For some of the children we work with, there will be separation due to a parent being in prison. The feelings and concerns around a parent being in a prison can be huge for the family, and it can carry with it feelings of shame, guilt and embarrassment. Many families find it very hard to know how to tell a child and what to tell a child. The Family Lives website has some useful information for families,[7] including a range of leaflets looking at:

- the impact of imprisonment on other family members

- living with separation

---

7   www.familylives.org.uk/search/?searchType=phrase&keywords=
in+prison&siid=19

- preparing for release

- the impact of parent imprisonment on the mental health of children and young people

- how to tell children about the imprisonment.

If this situation arises in your setting, it is important for staff to read around the issue, and be available to support the child and family. The charity Barnardo's delivers work around supporting families and prisoners with children; they have a briefing paper that describes their work and how they support families.[8] The paper is based on their work in Northern Ireland, but they deliver similar work across the UK.

There are a few children's books about parents in prison:

- *My Dad's in Prison* by Jackie Walter.

- *Danny's Mum* by Lesley Saddington.

- *Tommy's Dad* by Emma Randle-Caprez.

The feelings and confusion a child may feel due to family separation, whether through parents separating or a parent in prison, can last for a while, and we need to remember that just because the change happened a few months ago, this may not mean the child is used to it or at ease with it. As early years practitioners, we need to keep in mind what the child has experienced and is experiencing.

References

Cole, B. (2000) *Two of Everything*. London: Red Fox.

Krasny Brown, L. and Brown, M. (1988) *Dinosaurs Divorce: A Guide for Changing Families*. London: Little Brown.

Masurel, C. (2002) *Two Homes*. London: Walker Books.

Randle-Caprez, E. (2005) *Tommy's Dad*. Action for Prisoners Families.

Saddington, L. (2005) *Danny's Mum*. Action for Prisoners Families.

---

8   www.barnardos.org.uk/pp_no_8_when_a_parent_goes_to_prison.pdf

Thomas, P. (2014) *My Family's Changing: A First Look at Family Breakdown.* London: Wayland.

Walter, J. (2018) *My Dad's in Prison.* London: Franklin Watts.

Chapter 9

Illness and Hospital Stays

This chapter is going to explore how we can support children when they become ill and need to go to hospital or when a parent becomes ill. Serious illness is not always something we can prepare for; however, sometimes it is possible to plan for hospital stays and the changes that occur around illness.

Going to hospital

Staying in hospital is a massive change for children – even if it is only as a day patient, the experience will be very different to the child's normal day. It is so helpful for the child and family when they can be prepared and supported to know what will happen. Early years practitioners can support children and families in this – you don't need to be an expert in knowing what will happen, but, by having some knowledge, being able to signpost families and offer support is helpful to the child and family.

There is a charity called What? Why? Children in Hospital that has produced a film called *How Do You Prepare for Hospital.*[1] The hospital psychologist on this film, Jannie Donnan, explains how we know that

---

1   www.whatwhychildreninhospital.org.uk/video-prepare-for-hospital

children are helped when they are prepared in advance for going into hospital. She emphasizes how important it is for children to be told about the hospital visit and to be given enough information for their age and understanding, which helps them to know what to expect. It is really important for early years practitioners to remember this, as we may be working with families where they think it will be better for the children if they are not told beforehand, because they do not want to scare the children. However, we can support parents to know and understand how we need to help the child to feel prepared and help them to understand what is going to happen.

A planned hospital stay or visit

When a child has a planned visit or stay in hospital for a procedure, they will be invited in before the visit to see the hospital play specialists, who will talk them through the process. The play specialists use toys and books and real equipment to help the child understand what will happen. Many play specialists are now using Medibears[2] or something similar. These are soft toy bears that have had medical equipment fitted to them (e.g. a cannula), and they help the child to understand the procedure they are going to have. The play specialists are also available when the child returns for treatment; they can support in the preparation before the procedure and are available to help children to play after afterwards.

Hospitals use a wide range of resources to help children feel prepared for what is going to happen. In Glasgow, they have a teddy bear hospital that takes children through the different procedures they may have. In Bristol, they have a mini scanner that a small doll can go into. In Scotland, they use the Hospital Passport: Coping Kit.[3] This is a resource for all families to use with the child, and it includes

---

2   www.bbc.co.uk/news/av/uk-england-norfolk-46794916/medibears-help-children-at-norfolk-and-norwich-hospital

3   www.knowledge.scot.nhs.uk/media/CLT/ResourceUploads/4029791/Hospital%20Passport%20MKN%20Slides%20240613.pdf

information for the medical staff about the child, which the child and parents can fill in (this is similar to the all-about-me kit that we use in early years in England). This pack also has some Bright Ideas Cards, which offer ideas about what might help the child when they are in hospital (e.g. taking in a few toys or calming exercises they can do).

Preparation through play

We know that play is the way children work through and think about the changes they are encountering or experiences they are having. Most early years settings will have hospital play kits. These can be great, but often they are not very realistic; however, you could consider adding to the items you already have. Consider getting some bandages, tape, plasters, a real syringe, gloves, a mask, a surgeon's hat. When children have the opportunity to play with these real items, it can help them to become more familiar with the things they are going to see in hospital and it can help them to process the fears and anxiety they may be feeling. Alongside the medical tools have a doll or stuffed animal that the child can use within the play if they want.

As with all excellent early years practice, the play needs to be child-led – it can be good to have adults alongside to support, but it is vital that the child is given the space to explore and play in the way they want. You could also include other hospital-themed toys in your provision – Playmobil® have a variety of hospital play sets, including an X-ray machine and a paediatrician set, which includes weighing scales and a height measurer. If you have a child in your setting who returns to you and has a visual change (e.g. a feeding tube or a limb in a plaster cast), you could consider adapting one of your soft toys to have a cast or tube fitted. There are various examples of people who have done this. A woman in Glasgow has been adapting teddies to help children get used to the new medical changes they are experiencing.[4] If a teddy has a real tube fitted, it helps children to understand that this is ok; it helps them and their friends to see and learn about it, and explore the tubes without hurting the child.

Resources for children

Hospitals have been producing some fantastic resources to help children. Bristol Children's Hospital have made a film called *A Little Deep Sleep* about having an anaesthetic.[5] It's a lovely child-friendly film that talks through what will happen and who the child will see. It uses children's voices to narrate the film, and as part of the production they interviewed children about their experiences. The website What? Why? Children in Hospital has a wide range of films for different aged children talking about different experiences of hospital,[6] including blood tests, ECGs and general anaesthetics. All of these videos include children and adults having the procedure and talking about it.

Another film by Bristol Children's Hospital called *One of a Kind* is an animated film about how radiotherapy works, and is again narrated by a child.[7] This film may also be useful for a child to watch if their parent is having radiotherapy. All these films are about offering children some ideas and preparation for how the experience of being in hospital will be for them. I think these films will also offer parents some reassurance as well.

As an early years practitioner, if you have a child in your setting who is going to hospital, it is worth looking at these films, and being familiar with them. By watching the films yourself, you

4   www.bbc.co.uk/news/uk-scotland-glasgow-west-47123611
5   www.uhbristol.nhs.uk/patients-and-visitors/your-hospitals/bristol-royal-hospital-for-children/childrens-website/operations-and-tests/going-to-theatre
6   www.whatwhychildreninhospital.org.uk/videos-all
7   www.uhbristol.nhs.uk/patients-and-visitors/your-hospitals/bristol-royal-hospital-for-children/patient-and-family-support-services/one-of-a-kind

are then able to talk to the child about what they will encounter, you are able to use the correct words, and you are also in a better position to support the families.

There is also a variety of books you can share with children about going into hospital. Some of the ones I like are:

- *Usborne First Experiences: Going to the Hospital* by Anna Civardi.

- *A Little Princess Story: I Don't Want to Go to Hospital* by Tony Ross.

- *The Big Day! Going to Hospital* by Nicola Barber.

- *Talking It Through: Hospital* by Althea Braithwaite.

A parent's illness

For some children in your setting, the illness and hospital stay will be linked with a parent's ill health. Sometimes this can be prepared for, when parents know ahead they will be having a hospital stay, but of course other times this can be a sudden and unplanned experience. Wherever possible, it is again important to prepare children. When a parent is ill, this can put a huge strain on the whole family, and it might have a financial implication as well causing emotional turmoil.

If the hospital visit is planned, the early years setting can help the family to think about ways to support and prepare the child. As I have suggested in previous chapters, giving children the chance to process the information and the opportunity to ask questions is so important. It is vital to give children information that they can understand. It is likely they already realize that something is wrong. An example of words you could use is *'Daddy has an illness called cancer, it is making him feel very poorly. He still loves you and he wants to give you hugs, but he is too poorly to be able to run and chase with you at the moment. The doctors are trying to make him better.'* Sometimes, it is easier for early years practitioners to have these ongoing conversations with children as they don't have the emotional connection that the parents may be carrying. Of course, the news needs to come first of all from the family, but the early years setting can continue to explore this a bit more with the child. The Marie Curie website has a useful fact sheet about how to tell children, when to tell children and what to tell children.[8]

Supporting families in ill health

If it is known that the ill health is going to be long term, as an early years setting you need to consider if you can signpost the family to other services that may be able to help them. Your local children's centre or Citizens Advice service should be able to offer support and advice regarding financial support the family may be entitled to.

Preparing the child

As I discussed earlier, when a child has a planned hospital stay they will have the opportunity to visit the hospital and meet the plays specialists and maybe some of the medical staff before the procedure. If the parent is going in hospital, the preparation is not the same for the child. However, there are some things the family and early years setting could do to help. You could use the same books about going to hospital, but explain that it will be the parent; in the same way, you could also make sure there are play materials to explore and play with. You could also make a social story about the parent going to hospital. The social story could include photos of the hospital, hospital staff in their uniform and the parent, and, if you know that the parent is going to be attached to wires or a machine, you could include a photo of these. Early years practitioners could write one of these for the family, with their permission.

---

8   www.mariecurie.org.uk/help/support/diagnosed/family-friends/children #whoshouldtellchildren

CASE EXAMPLE

I recently wrote a social story for a young family where there were two daughters aged two and four, and their mum had been rushed to hospital and was in a coma. At first, the children were told she was poorly but were given limited further details. Understandably, the girls were very confused. When the mum came out of the coma, the plan was for the girls to visit, but she was still seriously ill and attached to various machines.

I wrote a very simple social story to prepare the girls for seeing their mum in such an alien environment. The story I wrote talked about how their mummy was very poorly, it described how the doctors and nurses were looking after her. I explained that she needed some machines and special medicine to help her get better; the medicine was going into her body from a tube, but this didn't hurt her and it was helping her. I finished by telling them that their mummy loved them very much and was looking forward to seeing them. The story included photos of the girls and their mum before she was ill, photos of doctors and nurses in their uniform and of a hospital bed with machines by it.

This story was shared with the girls a few times before they went to the hospital. It enabled them to be prepared for what they were going to see and allowed them to ask questions. It is very frightening to have your parent suddenly taken into hospital, and increasingly so when the parent has wires and machines attached to them.

If the parent is suffering from a significant illness that means they will need ongoing treatment or recuperation, it is important that this is explained to the children. This is very hard for children to understand, but it is so much better for them to be told information that they can begin to process, rather than not being told. As I mentioned in an earlier chapter, sometimes parents who have a serious illness don't tell the children, but often the children know that something is wrong, and not having the correct information and support around this can be extremely scary.

Books

Books are such a useful way of beginning to find the words to tell a child when a parent is ill. This is such a difficult area – parents' emotions will be very high and they will be feeling very sensitive, but they want to use the right words. There are a few books that explain about illness of adult relatives, but unfortunately most of them are based around grandparents being ill. This is good when it is a grandparent who is ill, but sometimes it is the parent, and they are not old, and using a book about a grandparents being ill can be confusing for children and can make it difficult for them to understand. I personally think there needs to be more books written for young children about parental illness. Examples of a few that are available are:

- *Mummy's Lump* by Gillian Forest – a book gently explaining breast cancer. This is beautifully and sensitively written and is available free on Kindle.

- *Grandma* by Jessica Shepherd – a book about a grandparent with dementia who needs to go into a care home.

- *Mummy's Got Bipolar* by Sonia Mainstone-Cotton.

- *The Colour Thief* by Andrew Fusek Peters and Polly Peters – a family story of depression written for slightly older children.

References

Barber, N. (2011) *The Big Day! Going to Hospital.* London: Wayland.

Braithwaite, A. (2000) *Talking It Through: Hospital.* Manningtree: Happy Cat Books.

Civardi. A. (2005) *Usborne First Experiences: Going to the Hospital.* London: Usborne.

Forrest, G. (2015) *Mummy's Lump.* London: Breast Cancer Care.

Fusek Peters, A. and Peters, P. (2015) *The Colour Thief: A Family's Story of Depression.* London: Wayland.

Mainstone-Cotton, S. (2017) *Mummy's Got Bipolar.* Bath: Jonson.

Ross. T (2000) *A Little Princess Story: I Don't Want to Go to Hospital.* London: Anderson Press.

Shepherd. J. (2014) *Grandma.* Swindon: Child's Play Library.

Chapter 10

Death and Bereavement

Death and bereavement is such a difficult area to think about. I have supported a few children through bereavement over the years, but I am certainly not an expert in this area. For this chapter, I consulted with a friend of mine, Will Taylor,[1] who specializes in counselling for children who have experienced loss and bereavement. I want to give a wellbeing warning for this chapter: it is of course a very emotive subject, and if this is too painful right now for you to read, then be kind to yourself – it is ok to skip it.

As an early years practitioner, you are very likely at some point to have children in your setting who will experience death and bereavement. Every 22 minutes a parent with dependent children dies in the UK, up to 70 per cent of schools have a bereaved child in their school, and 92 per cent of young people will experience a significant bereavement before the age of 16.[2] The subject of death and bereavement brings about so many challenging feelings and emotions for staff. It is so important that you protect yourself as staff, that you take note of your own feelings and get the appropriate support.

---

1   http://willtaylor.online
2   www.childbereavementuk.org/early-years-supporting-bereaved-children

This is an area where, sometimes, you can prepare a child for the death, but there will be occasions when it is not possible; for example, in the case of sudden death. This is also an area where it may be important to signpost the family and the child to other agencies that specialize in this area, and I will direct you to some organizations at the end of the chapter. However, it is important to remember that in our roles we can all offer support; as the charity Child Bereavement UK says, 'Most grieving children do not need a "bereavement expert" they need people who care.'[3]

Talking about death

In the UK, we are particularly poor at talking about death. How often have we heard people use the words 'they have passed away', 'we have lost them', 'they have gone to a better place', 'they are no longer with us', 'they passed', and 'they have gone to sleep'. This is so unhelpful, particularly for children – the statements are ambiguous, leaving questions and uncertainty. A child hearing that their parent is lost will be led to think they will come back; if they hear that they have gone to a better place, this may lead them to think the person didn't want to be with them; if they hear that the person has gone to sleep, they will naturally assume the person will wake up. Children need to know what has happened and that the person is not coming back; we need to use the word *death*.

With early years children, adults often presume they are too young to understand and therefore we don't need to tell them. However, as early years practitioners, we know that children under the age of five are processing so much information; they are curious and inquisitive and they will know that something is wrong and something significant has changed. We need to ensure that we are honest and clear with children and not shy away from using the word *death*. Whatever your own or the families' views are around

---

3   www.childbereavementuk.org/Pages/Category/early-years

death or an afterlife, children still need to know that death means they will not see the person again; they are not about to reappear.

As early years practitioners working with the family, we are in a position to sensitively offer some thoughts and we are able to signpost families. Before you use the word *death* with a child, you will of course need to find out from the family what they have said, what words they have used. If the family are telling you they have not used the word *death*, I would encourage you to talk to them about the importance of using this word.

Young children's understanding

It will be difficult for a child under the age of five to understand the idea of death being final, particularly for a younger child. You may find they repeat a question about when are they seeing the person or when is the person coming home. In these situations, they need a gentle reminder that the person has died and they are not coming home. This can be so hard for family members, as they can feel they are having to repeat the painful words numerous times. Child Bereavement UK has a very useful guidance sheet about the different ages children understand death.[4] The guidance is that a child under the age of two has no understanding, but they will react to changes in the environment experienced by the loss of a significant person. Children between the ages of two and five are aware of the idea of death and begin to be aware that dead is different to living, although they do not understand the idea of the permanence of death.

---

4   www.childbereavementuk.org/Handlers/Download.ashx?IDMF=6c118a29
-2f1a-4024-ba9e-c44701b1ff3e

When we know someone is going to die

In many situations, it will be known that someone is going to die, allowing some time for planning and preparation. Again, sometimes adults are afraid to tell a child that a person is dying; they are afraid that this is too confusing for them and want to protect the child from this difficult news. However, children will know something is wrong, they will recognize that people are behaving differently or even recognize that the atmosphere around them has changed. If they do not have an explanation for this, they can become very agitated and afraid; they may fear they have done something wrong and it is their fault.

Finding the words to tell a child that someone is dying is of course incredibly hard and painful. Younger children just need simple words and a gentle explanation. In the previous chapter, I wrote about the importance of talking to a child about their parent's illness, using simple words such as *'Daddy has an illness called cancer, it is making him feel very poorly. He still loves you and he wants to give you hugs, but he is too poorly to be able to run and chase with you at the moment. The doctors are trying to make him better.'* If a child already knows that the parent is ill, you can then build on this to tell them that the person is going to die.

Child Bereavement UK suggest you build on what the child already knows,[5] so you could say *'You know that Daddy has been very poorly with cancer, and he can't run and play with you. The doctors have been trying to make him better but the medicine is not working, Daddy is going to die, we are not sure when but we think it will be soon. That means he won't be with us any more.'* This is of course incredibly difficult for a child to understand, but it is so important that they have the chance to hear this and begin to process it before the event happens.

---

5   www.childbereavementuk.org/when-someone-is-not-expected-to-live

How children respond

Responses from a child will be very varied, because under-fives will struggle with the idea of death being final, and they may not react initially. Parents can find this upsetting or confusing, but early years practitioners are in a position to reassure them that this is not because the child doesn't care, it is because the child doesn't yet understand about how death is final. It is also not unusual for children to show a wide range of behaviours, but sadness may not be the immediate response. A child may start to display challenging behaviour, become very clingy, have their sleep affected, or appear to regress. These are all very normal behaviours in this situation, and parents and practitioners need to remember that this is the child's way of showing you that they are troubled by what has happened.

The Marie Curie website explains how children can appear to alternate quickly between grieving, being sad and getting on with their normal lives.[6] They describe this as 'puddle jumping' – the puddle is their grief and they are quickly in and out of the puddle. I think, for early years children, this is a really good description. As I mentioned before, a child may repeatedly ask the same question, such as *'When is Daddy coming home?'* They may also ask if they are going to die, if you are going to die, if their sister is going to die, etc. They need lots of reassurance that you are not going to die, and that it is not their fault.

How the early years setting can support the child and family

When we have a child that we work with who has experienced a bereavement, particularly a close bereavement, we need to acknowledge what has happened, and the key person in an early years setting will be the most appropriate adult to do this. When

---

6 www.mariecurie.org.uk/help/support/bereaved-family-friends/supporting
-grieving-child/grief-affect-child

we first see the child after the event we need to say *'I am sorry that ... died. That is very sad.'* Remind them you are there for them – you could say, *'I am here for you, come and tell me if you need a hug.'*

I always recommend that schools and early years settings have a bereavement policy. In this you will talk about who will contact the family and how you will support the child and family (e.g. if a parent of the child has died, are you going to go to the funeral, are you going to send flowers or a card to the family?). In the moment of death, particularly if it is a sudden death, it can be so hard to know what to do; what is the right thing to do. If you have thought this through previously, you can refer to your policy in the moment when you may be in shock. These policies are also essential for the event of a member of staff dying or a child in your setting dying, giving you guidance on knowing what to do in a very hard situation. There are a few places where you can find some advice on how to write a bereavement policy. The charity Cruse has a page on their website with suggestions,[7] and Child Bereavement UK has an example on their website of an early years policy.[8]

At this time of massive change and emotional distress, it is so important that the child has a familiar safe routine at the early years setting. Their world will be rocked, and they need something to remain constant. This should be discussed in team meetings and supervision, giving particular thought to ensuring that routines stay the same and carefully thinking through any possible changes that lie ahead, remembering that the smallest of changes could be overwhelming for the child. The child especially needs staff to be loving, caring, consistent and nurturing. You may find that the child is more in need of staying close to their key person, or they may be more tired than usual – sometimes when children are very stressed they become more tired. Staff need to be aware of this and provide the appropriate resources in the early years setting, such as ensuring

---

7   www.cruse.org.uk/get-help/for-schools/school-bereavement-policy
8   www.childbereavementuk.org/early-years-bereavement-policy

that you have a quiet space with cushions and maybe a tented area where the child can retreat if they want to

When the death is through suicide

This is an especially difficult area. The family are dealing with the shock of a sudden death, but also the way the person has died is very distressing. This can often leave the family feeling shocked, overwhelmed, sometimes feeling guilty and sometimes feeling angry. Alongside having the feeling of loss, the family may also be having to answer difficult questions and may feel judgement from others.

Suicide is such a difficult subject to explain to children. Winston's Wish have published a guidance book on this called *Beyond the Rough Rock*. They also have a page on their website about suicide and a helpline for advice.[9] As early years practitioners, we need to keep in mind that the family will be experiencing a wide range of emotions; we need to ensure that we are calm, caring and non-judgemental to them, providing them with a safe space where they know their child will be loved and nurtured in this difficult time.

Attending funerals

Children attending funerals seems to cause a huge range of emotions, with some people believing they absolutely shouldn't and other people believing they absolutely should.

My children attended the funeral of their great-grandparents and great aunt when they were between three and five years old. Interestingly, now at 20 and 22 they both remember the funerals and comment on how, when they look back, they are pleased they went. For me, it felt the right thing to do – they knew and loved the people who died and they are an important part of the wider family, I felt

---

9   www.winstonswish.org/when-someone-in-your-family-dies-by-suicide

they had a right to be there. From a practical side, I think it helped having them there, they brought a relief and lightness to the day.

Attending funerals enables a child to say goodbye, and funerals are an important part of the process of saying goodbye. If the child is old enough to make the decision about whether they want to attend or not, then adults need to support them in making this decision by giving them information about what will happen and what they can expect. With under-fives I would say this is too abstract a choice for a child to make; however, I do think there is huge value in having the child at the funeral. Winston's Wish have a page on their website offering advice around this.[10] Early years practitioners may be asked about this by the family, and it is worth looking at the suggested web pages and signposting them to parents.

Resources
Books for children

Books are such an important tool when we are supporting children through death and bereavement. There are a growing range of books now available, some of the ones I would recommend are:

- *Goodbye Mousie* by Robie Harris.

- *I Miss You: A First Look at Death* by Pat Thomas.

- *Is Daddy Coming Back in a Minute?* by Elke Barber and Alex Barber.

- *What Happened to Daddy's Body?* by Elke Barber and Alex Barber.

---

10   www.winstonswish.org/attending-the-funeral

Books for adults to support children

- *Muddles, Puddles and Sunshine* from Winston's Wish – this is a book with ideas of activities that an adult can do with a child to support them through the grieving process. It is aimed at slightly older children, but it has ideas you could adapt.

- *Beyond the Rough Rock* from Winston's Wish – this book is about helping families who have experienced suicide.

- *Never Too Young to Grieve* from Winston's Wish – this book is about supporting children under the age of five who are bereaved.

Places where you can get help as professional and signpost to parents

- Winston's Wish: www.winstonswish.org – they also have a free helpline for families or professionals: 08088 020 021

- Marie Curie: www.mariecurie.org.uk – they also have a free helpline for families who are experiencing terminal illness or death: 0800 090 2309

- Child Bereavement UK: www.childbereavementuk.org – support for families and professionals; they have a free helpline: 0800 02 888 40

I am going to finish this chapter with an example of what I consider to be an inspiring way in which one woman helped the children she worked with understand her death.

CASE EXAMPLE – HELPING CHILDREN UNDERSTAND DEATH

A head teacher of a nursery and primary school in the city I work in died of cancer recently. Her name was Sue East – she was a friend of mine and was a huge character. Sue had cancer, and the return of the cancer and then her death ended up being quite quick. When Sue went into the hospice and knew she was dying, she wrote the children of the school a letter.[11] The letter was to be read in assembly, to the whole school.

The letter told them she was going to die soon. She told them how amazing they all were and how amazing the school was. She thanked them for sharing their joy and friendship and explained it was time for her to move on to new adventures, to the peace of heaven. This letter ended up going viral on the internet. I think this was a wonderful example of an incredibly special woman showing us how to support children to not be afraid about death and how to help them understand what was happening. She knew it was important that the children heard from her that she was dying.

She died a few days after writing this letter. The whole school were then also involved in her funeral; the children sang a song, accompanied by staff and parents and old pupils. The children drew pictures for her cardboard coffin, and made paper flowers for every person in the funeral to wave as she was carried out of the abbey at the end of the service. Everyone who knew Sue was upset by her death; however, it was an incredible experience to be in a full abbey with many, many children along with adults, being able to share together and celebrate her life.

---

11   www.somersetlive.co.uk/in-your-area/st-andrews-bath-sue-east-2411348

References

Barber, A. and Barber, E. (2016) *Is Daddy Coming Back in a Minute: Explaining (Sudden) Death in Words Very Young Children Can Understand.* London: Jessica Kingsley Publishers.

Barber, A. and Barber, E. (2016) *What Happened to Daddy's Body? Explaining What Happens After Death in Words Very Young Children Can Understand.* London: Jessica Kingsley Publishers.

Harris, R. (2004) *Goodbye Mousie.* New York, NY: Aladdin Paperbacks.

Thomas, P. (2009) *I Miss You: A First Look at Death.* London: Wayland.

Winston's Wish (2008) *Beyond the Rough Rock.* Cheltenham: Winston's Wish.

Winston's Wish (2009) *Muddles, Puddles and Sunshine.* Stroud: Hawthorn Press.

Winston's Wish (2018) *Never Too Young to Grieve.* Cheltenham: Winston's Wish.

Conclusion

Managing change is part of life. Children will experience many changes throughout their lives – some of these changes will be fun and exciting and others will be life-changing and potentially traumatic. As early years practitioners, we are in a unique position to help, guide and support a child and family through the changes they experience. However, to do this we need to keep in mind that change can be hard, and even small changes can be unsettling. We need to continue to think and reflect on how we can support children through these changes.

I have only covered a few changes and transitions that children experience, but hopefully these have given you ideas and thoughts about how you can continue to support families and support children's wellbeing.

Thank you for taking the time to read this.

Index

by the same author

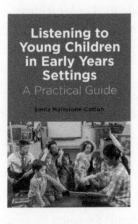

Listening to Young Children in Early Years Settings
A Practical Guide
Sonia Mainstone-Cotton

Paperback: £14.99 / $22.95
ISBN: 978 1 78592 469 9
eISBN: 978 1 78450 855 5
120 pages

It is widely accepted that listening to and involving children in decisions about their care, learning and development can significantly improve the quality of early years provision. This book gives practical guidance on how to do this effectively.

Starting with a discussion about why we listen to children and the policies around this, the book explains how we can involve children in decision-making that is appropriate to their age and level of understanding. Packed full of examples and ideas that can be easily applied in practice, it covers how to listen to children's perspectives and involve them in staff recruitment and appraisals, classroom design, assessment processes for social services and EHC plans, and much more.

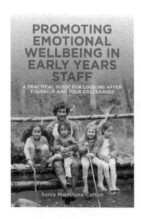

**Promoting Emotional Wellbeing
in Early Years Staff**
**A Practical Guide for Looking after
Yourself and Your Colleagues**
Sonia Mainstone-Cotton

Paperback: £14.99 / $21.95
ISBN: 978 1 78592 335 7
eISBN: 978 1 78450 656 8
128 pages

Though children's wellbeing is high on the agenda for policy makers, the welfare of the professionals looking after them is often taken for granted. Sonia Mainstone-Cotton recognises that in order to enhance children's emotional wellbeing, it's vital that early years professionals are stress-free and emotionally well themselves. This is the first guide of its kind, offering succinct and practical guidance, tips and ideas for those working with young children on how to comfortably manage the pressures of their job, improve their work/ life balance, and support the wellbeing of their colleagues. Easy to dip in and out of, this guide is an essential item for any early years staff room.

Promoting Young Children's Emotional Health and Wellbeing
A Practical Guide for Professionals and Parents
Sonia Mainstone-Cotton

Paperback: £14.99 / $24.95
ISBN: 978 1 7859 2054 7
eISBN: 9781 7845 0311 6
168 pages

Positive emotional health in a child's earliest years can be a critical factor in their future development. Offering practical suggestions for games, activities and exercises designed to promote emotional wellbeing in young children, this essential guide showcases a wide range of approaches such as mindfulness and meditation, Forest School and Reggio Emilia to provide a hands-on reference for teachers and parents.

Drawing on over 25 years' experience as an early years professional, the author explores topics including playfulness, stillness, sensory play, creativity and staff wellbeing. Each topic references current best practices and international examples, and also includes a comprehensive list of further resources and activities. Providing an informative introduction to both theory and practice, this book demonstrates easy-to-implement ideas for any professional or parent engaging with young children.

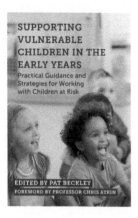

**Supporting Vulnerable
Children in the Early Years**
Practical Guidance and Strategies
for Working with Children at Risk
Edited by Pat Beckley
Foreword by Professor Chris Atkin

Paperback: £16.99 / $24.95
ISBN: 978 1 7859 2237 4
eISBN: 978 1 7845 0515 8
272 pages

Exploring specific experiences, circumstances and events that can put children at risk, this book provides practical guidance for early years practitioners working with vulnerable children. It covers supporting children who are abused and neglected, those with special educational needs, children from ethnic minorities, those with emotional or health difficulties, children affected by poverty and children in care.

Each chapter draws on current research and theories to set out clear advice and strategies for supporting the wellbeing and development of vulnerable children, including working in partnership with parents, carers and communities.

Pat Beckley is Senior Lecturer for Early Years at Bishop Grosseteste University, Lincoln, UK. She has published numerous books for early years practitioners, including *Effective Early Years Leadership* and *The New Early Years Foundation Stage*.